Ralls County Missouri

Settlement Records

1832–1853

Sherida K. Eddlemon

HERITAGE BOOKS
2010

HERITAGE BOOKS

AN IMPRINT OF HERITAGE BOOKS, INC.

Books, CDs, and more—Worldwide

For our listing of thousands of titles see our website
at
www.HeritageBooks.com

Published 2010 by
HERITAGE BOOKS, INC.
Publishing Division
100 Railroad Ave. #104
Westminster, Maryland 21157

International Standard Book Numbers
Paperbound: 978-1-55613-821-8
Clothbound: 978-0-7884-8570-1

PREFACE

Ralls County was created November 16, 1820 from Pike County. The County was named for Missouri legislator, Daniel Ralls.

The genealogical abstracts contained in this volume are taken from Roll No. C5637 obtained from the Missouri State Archives. Copies of the original may be obtained for a small fee from the Missouri State Archives, Office of Secretary of State, Capitol Building, Jefferson City, Missouri, 65101.

Every effort has been made to retain the original spelling of names and any other genealogical data included with the settlement record. The information included varies from settlement to settlement. Some settlements give the names of heirs, disposition of property, funeral dates, while others give nothing but a date with just voucher numbers without names. Dates which help establish an approximate time of death or burial are included; however such dates are few. All entries are in the order as they appear in the original records. In some cases it appears that the actual record was recorded much later than the filing date.

Some abbreviations have been used in this volume. They are as follows:

RD	-	Recorded Date
FD	-	Filed Date
CLK	-	County Clerk
DPY	-	Deputy County Clerk
dec	-	Deceased
adm	-	Administrator
exr	-	Executor

Hopefully, you may find your ancestor within these pages.

Ralls County, Missouri, Settlements, Vol. A, 1832 - 1850,
Roll No. 5637.
1) Final settlement of James L. Caldwell, adm., of the
estate of Green Caldwell, dec.
Monies Received: Dabney Jones (Case of Porter Vs. Jones),
P. M. Glen, Fielding Combs, Robert Jefferies, Oney Carstarp-
hen. (RD) February 14, 1832, (CLK) Charles Glascock.
Cash received at second annual settlement: Morgan Paris,
B.F. Saunders, Willis M. Jamison, Jacob Asher, Robert Burns,
Hamilton Fike, Jonathan Abby, jr., James G. Wiley.
Monies Expended: James Rappin, Oney Carstarphen, William
Brandon, Dabney Jones.
Money expended at the second annual settlement: James C.
Barnett, George W. Pierce, Charless & Pascal, John W. Cama,
Harvey Smith, John Curry, Z. O. Fraper, Gabriel B. Reed, Wm.
Sprat, Coleman D. Stone, William Wilcoxen, D. M. Lane, John
Gray, James Mappin, David Watson, Henry Smelser, Margaret
Brandon, John A. Bowman, Joshua S. Eli, L. Rogers, Asa Glas-
cock.
2) Annual settlement of William Crawford, adm. of the
estate of James Crawford, dec. February term, 1834.
Monies Expended: John M. Hager, Robert Crawford, John
Crawford. (RD) February 11, 1834, (CLK) Charles Glascock.
(DPY) Harrison Glascock.
3) Settlement of Branch Hatcher, adm., of the estate of
Stephen P. Cook., February term, 1834.
Slaves: Slave, Milla, appraised at $175 died. Girl sla-
ve, Sidney, appraised at $175, negro boy, Moses, valued at
$300, negro boy, Dan, appraised at $275. Negro boy, Daniel,
was hired out in 1833. Robert Lyle and S. M. Prewitt hired
negroes from the estate.
Monies Expended: Schooling for Elizabeth Cook. Clothing
for Milla, a slave.
4) John Jamison and Jane Fisher, adm. of the estate of
Sidney S. Fisher, dec. No name listed in settlement. (RD)
May 7, 1834, (CLK) Charles Glascock, (DPY) Harrison Glascock
5) John Jamison and Andromicha Jamison, adm., estate of
William Jamison, dec. May term, 1834.
Monies Received: Joel Rowley, Simon Davis, Edmund Hyde,
Lewis Tracy.
Monies Expended: Thomas S. Barkley, Abel M. Connor, John
Ross, Dabney Jones, Charles Glascock, Thomas A. Pardom, Wm.
S. Lofland, Lewis Tracy, Handford Brown. (RD) May 7, 1834,
(CLK) Charles Glascock, (DPY) Harrison Glascock.
6) James D. Caldwell, adm., of the estate of Green Cald-
well, dec., February term, 1835.
Monies Received: R. Caldwell & Co.
Monies Expended: R. Caldwell & Co., R. L. Samuel, A. B.
Chambers, W. Culbertson as adm. of L. Peter. (RD) February

1

5, 1835, (CLK) Charles Glascock.

7) Annual settlement of Turner Haden, adm. of Benonia Haden, dec., February term, 1835.

Monies Expended: Chambers & Harris, Wm. Fisher, George Fisher, D. Jones. (CLK) Charles Glascock, (RD) February 9, 1835, (DPY) Harrison Glascock, (JP) W. S Lofland.

8) Settlement of Branch Hatcher, adm. of S.P. Cook, dec. Slaves: Daniel, Moses, Liddy.

Monies Expended: Shoes for Elizabeth Cook from R. Lane of Palmyra. (RD) February 10, 1835, (CLK) Charles Glascock, (DPY) Harrison Glascock.

9) Settlement of John Jamison, adm. for the estate of Sydney S. Fisher. February term, 1835.

Monies Received: Saml. H. Hill, Jas. Smith, jr., J. A. Boarman, James D. Caldwell, Chapel Castarphen, J. S. Fisher, sr., Stephen Cleaver, Lewis Tracy, R. King.

Monies Expended: F.H. Stewart, L. Tracy, J.L. Fisher, R. King, J. Ralls, C. Glascock, A. M. Connor, J. D. Caldwell, (RD) February 10, 1835, (CLK) Charles Glascock, (DPY) Harrison Glascock.

10) Annual settlement of Wilkinson Crawford, adm. of Jas. Crawford, dec., February term, 1835.

Monies Expended: Dr.Lyle. (RD) February 10, 1835, (CLK) Charles Glascock, (DPY) Harrison Glascock.

11) John Jamison and Andromecha Jamison, adm., of estate of William Jameson, dec., May term, 1835.

Monies Received: David A. Briggs, Volney Brewer, William H. Flowrence, Jas. Ritchey, Jos. Wright, Richard Epperson, Simon Davis, Jos. Alderidge, Daniel Brown, J. S. Crosthwait, John D. White.

Monies Expended: G. Arthur, J. D. Caldwell, Joseph Rice, Wm. Preast, H. A. Harris, J. J. Slosson, John D. White, R. Matson, Thos. A. Williams. James L. Fisher, E. Hant, S. W. Mayhall, Jas. Carson, John A. Boarman, Lake W. Watkins, John Ralls, Henry Smelster, James Patterson. (MD) May 6, 1835, (CLK) Charles Glascock, (DPY) Harrison Glascock.

12) Dabney Jones and Francis Conn, extrs. of the estate of James Ledford, dec. August term, 1835.

Monies Received: S. W. Maryhall, Nancy Ledford, Abraham Buford, William O. Young, George Jefferies,Oney Carstarphen, Joel Ledford, Robert Weldy, Robert Briggs, R. S. Howard, Daniel Ledford.

Monies Expended: F. Conn, D. Jones, Joseph Berry, James Ledford, John M. Turley, J. D. Caldwell, Joshua Bosley, A.B. Chambers, James Busby, A. Wright, Joseph Wright, William O. Young, Francis Conn, J. A. Boarman. (RD) August 6, 1835, (CLK) Charles Glascock, (DPY) Harrison Glascock.

13) Annual settlement of Joseph D. Tapley, adm. of the estate of Green Tapley, dec. November term, 1835.

Monies Received: Charles Glascock, Lewis Tracy, A. Davis, Philip Briscoe, David Briggs, W. Mary, Lewis Batthrope, Jos. Fisher, Walker Carter, Richard Brashears, R. S. Howard, Wm. Sims, Jacob Ashurst, S. Winn, Benjamin Livers, Jos. Fanning, Walter Caldwell, Robert Caldwell, Saml. Hill, Saml. K. Caldwell.

Monies Expended: John Shulse, Gabriel Philips, William S. Gant, C. B. Sinclair, Thos. Cleaver, Stephen Cleaver, Dabney Jones, Chambers & Harris,Simon Davis, John Tracy, Dr. McCoy, James & J. Simmitts, Lyra Haden, Wm. Jones for J. Stephens, P.M. Glenn, Dr. Jett, David O. Glascock, Joseph Fannin, John Lockwood. (RD) November 3, 1835, (CLK) Charles Glasck, (DPY) Harrison Glascock.

14) Settlement of Branch Hatcher, adm. of S.P. Cook. February term, 1836.

Slaves: Liddy, Moses, and Daniel were sold.

Monies Expended: B. Hatcher. Note: Money was still being paid out for schooling. (RD) February 2, 1836. (CLK) Harrison Glascock.

15) Annual settlement of Jeptha S. Croswaithe, admin. of the estate of Thomas Cathey.

No names given. (RD) February 3, 1836. (CLK) Harrison Glascock.

16) Final settlement of William Crawford, adm. of the estate of James Crawford. May term, 1836.

No names given. (RD) May 3,1836. (CLK) Harrison Glascock.

17) Final settlement of Abraham Seely, adm. of the estate of John N. Seely. May term. 1836.

Monies Received: Joel Ledford, Jeremiah Penix, Wm. James, James Smith, Thomas Ellis, John Lane, Absalom Ellis, J. C. Bowles, adm. of G. Wellay, dec., George Seely, --- Caldwell.

Monies Expended: A. Ledford, J. Williams, C. Glascock, H. Glascock, Chambers & Harris. Note: Funeral expenses were listed. (RD) May 6, 1836. (CLK) Harrison Glascock.

18) Fourth annual settlement of James D. Caldwell, adm. of Green V. Caldwell.

Monies Expended: Luke W. Watkins.

Monies Received: Balance of property in the firm of Robt. Caldwell and Green V. Caldwell not accounted for. A bond for Robert Caldwell has been posted with James Mapin, security. (RD) June 13, 1836, (CLK) Harrison Glascock.

19) Settlement of Richd. Boyce, adm. of estate of Spellsbury C. Garret.

Judgment: Money received of Edmund Hyde from judgment in Supreme Court.

Monies Expended: Uriel Wright, A.B. Chambers, H. Glascock. (RD) August 3, 1836, (CLK) Harrison Glascock.

20) Settlement of Dabney Jones and Francis Conn, adm. of the estate of James Ledford. August term, 1836.

3

Monies Received: William Hutcherson.
Monies Expended: James Chitwood, William D. Goodlow, Jas.
Carson, Absalom Ellis, Henry A. Harris. (RD) August 3, 1836,
(CLK) Harrison Glascock.
21) Annual settlement of George L. Hardy, admn. of the
estate of Arnold Hardy.
Monies Received: Jas. Alexander, Geo. L. Hardy. (RD) August 3, 1836, (CLK) Harrison Glascock.
22) Annual settlement of Mary Krigbaum, extrx. of Jacob
Krigbaum, dec.
Monies Received: John Tracy, Jos. Fanning.
Monies Expended: L.W. Watkins, adm. of Wm. S. Gant; Jas.
Cox. (RD) August 25, 1836, (CLK) Harrison Glascock.
23) Settlement of William Priest, exr. of the estate of
John Payne, dec.
Monies Received: B.N. Johnson, jr., Daniel Payne, Charles
Glascock.
Monies Expended: Lewis Tracy, J. Fanning, H. Brown. (RD)
November 7, 1836, (CLK) Harrison Glascock.
24) Annual settlement of Joseph D. Tapley, adm. of estate
of Green Tapley, dec.   November term, 1836.
Monies Received: Charles Scanland, Joseph D. Tapley, John
Tapley, Walter McFarland, James C. Barnett,James C. Garnett,
Luke W. Watkins.
Monies Expended: Rufus King, Chapel Carstarphen, Hannah
Tapley, B. A. Spaulding, Stephen Cleaver, Thomas A. Purdom,
Casey Forman, John Jones. (RD) November 7, 1836. (CLK) Harrison Glascock.
25) Annual settlement of French Glascock, adm. of Addison
Jeffers, dec.   November term, 1836.
Monies Received: J. C. Barnett, W. K. Flowrence, Richard
Matson, Chas. Glascock, Turner Priest, French Glascock, Tho.
Priest, James C. Barnett.
Monies Expended: Charles Glascock, Joshua Hope, L. Glascock, James L. Fisher, Hansford Brown, Turner G. Priest, Asa
Glascock, Richard Matson, Harrison Glascock, Harris & Chambers, Robert K. McCoy. (RD) November 8, 1836, (CLK) Harrison
Glascock. (RD) November 8, 1836, (CLK) Harrison Glascock.
26) Annual settlement of Macy Carisle, etrx. of Absalom
Carisle, dec.   November term, 1836.
No names given. (RD) November 9, 1836, (CLK) Harrison
Glascock.
27) Settlement of Luke W. Watkins, adm. of William S.
Grant.
Monies Received: Simon Davis,Jesse Kildreth,Asa Glascock,
Joshua Bosley, Posey Smith, Daniel Brown, Lewis Batthrope,
Russel King, Turner Priest, Joseph Fanning, John Brisco, C.
B. Sinclair, Rice Carter, Henry A. Harris, William Priest,

Thomas Dooley, John Byrne, N. R. Ledford, James Brown, Allin Brown, Joseph Fisher, William O. Young, Thomas Priest, Saml. W. Maryhall, David O. Glascock.

Monies Expended: Joshua Bosley, James D. Caldwell, Thomas Elder, Lewis Batthrope, Harrison Glascock, L. Batthrope, J. L. Wood, Len Porter, Philip Haley, Joseph Wright, Asa Glascock, R. King. (RD) November 9, 1836, (CLK) Harrison Glascock.

28) Annual settlement of John M. Johnson, adm. of John R. Dyke, dec. November term, 1836.

Monies Received: Richard Matson, Wm. Montgomery, Richard L. Howard.

Monies Expended: S. McGinis, Nash & Stone, James Conway, Willia, L. Shropshire, Harrison Glascock, Robert Stewart, J. W. Hayden, Buckannon N. Boyce, W. B. Rett, F. Glascock, R. Boyce, L. Rogers. (RD) November 9, 1837 (?) (CLK) Harrison Glascock.

29) Settlement of John Briscoe for the estate of Ralph D. Briscoe, dec. November term 1836.

Monies Expended: H. Glascock, Chambers & Harris. (RD) November 10, 1836, (CLK) Harrison Glascock.

30) John Jamison and Jane Fisher, admrs. of the estate of Sydney S. Fisher, dec. Third settlement.

Monies Expended: J. Croswaith, Wm. Hager, Harrison Glascock, Hansford Brown, Joshua Bosley, Jane Fisher, Chambers & Harris. (RD) November 10, 1836, (CLK) Harrison Glascock.

31) Jeptha A. Croswaithe, adm. of the estate of John F. Elliott, dec.

Monies Received: John Ralls, Isaac Bast, --- Brooks, John Tapley, --- Penn, L. Watkins, --- M'Kee, Moses Hawkins, John Jones, --- Keer, James Shohoney, Squire Brothers, Taylor Jones, Grey Carstarpehen, Wm. Cottendin, Stephen McPherson.

Monies Expended: Wm. O. Young, W. S. Lefland, Harrison Glascock. (RD) November 10, 1836, (CLK) Harrison Glascock.

32) John Jamison and Andromacha Jamison, adm. of the estate of William Jamison, dec. Third Settlement.

Monies Received: R. S. Howard, Thomas S. Barkley, Asa Glascock.

Monies Expended: Asa Glascock, Richard Matson, R. S. Howard, C. Carstarphen. (RD) November 10, 1836, (CLK) Harrison Glascock.

33) Morgan Paris, adm. of the estate of Moses Webb, dec. Final Settlement.

Monies Expended. J. Dales. (RD) February 6, 1837, (CLK) Harrison Glascock.

34) Final settlement of Joseph D. Tapley, adm. of the estate of Green Tapley, dec. February term, 1837.

Monies Received: H. Tapley, Joseph Fisher, Jonathan Hilbreth.

Slaves: Dinah, negro woman, died.
Monies Expended: Ezra Hunt, Chambers & Harris, L.W. Watkins.
35) Final settlement of French Glascock, adm. of Addison Jefferies, dec., February term, 1837.
Monies Expended: G. C. Hays, T. A. Pardom, Wm. Moss, Asa Glascock, Chambers & Harris, J. D. Caldwell, Maria Dodd. (RD) February 8, 1837, (CLK) Harrison Glascock.
36) Annual settlement of William Rogers, adm. of estate of Hamilton Rogers, dec. February, 1837.
Monies Expended: Wm. Blakey, Saml. Lefever, John Withers. (RD) February 8, 1837, (CLK) Harrison Glascock.
37) Annual settlement of Robert Weldy, adm. estate of George Weldey, dec.
No names given. (RD) March 9, 1837, (CLK) Harrison Glascock.
38) Final settlement of Charles Bohannan, adm. of the estate of James Bohannan, dec. May term, 1837.
No names given. (RD) May 1, 1837, (CLK) Harrison Glascock
39) Final settlement of Robert Weldy, adm. of George Wedly, dec. May term, 1837.
Monies Expended: N. Ledford, Chambers & Harris, W. O. Young, H. Glascock, P. Wright, W. Carson, H. Glascock.
40) Final settlement of Jonathan Abbey, adm. of the estate of George B. Abbey. May term, 1837.
No names given. (R) May 1, 1837, (CLK) Harrison Glascock
41) Final settlement of James D. Caldwell, adm. of Green V. Caldwell, dec.
Monies Expended: E. M. Holden, John Smith & brother, Harrison Glascock, --- Chambers. (RD) May 2, 1837, (CLK) Harrison Glascock.
42) Accounting of Richard Boyce, adm. of Spillsbury C. Garrent, dec. May term, 1837
No money expended or received. (RD) May 23, 1837, (CLK) Harrison Glascock
43) Final settlement of Turner Haden, adm. of Benonia Haden, dec. August term, 1837.
No names listed. (RD) August 7, 1837, (CLK) Harrison Glascock.
44) First annual settlement of Matthew Elliott, exr. of the estate Stephen Elliott, dec.
Monies Expended: Funeral expenses for May 17, 1836. Coffin expenses paid June 28th to George L. Hardy. Mentioned: Harrison Glascock, Hatton Hager, Benras (sic) J. Lynch, Wm. Harton, I. J. Lyle, Raphael Laeke. (RD) August 7, 1837, (CLK) Harrison Glascock.
45) Annual settlement of John Gaston, adm. of the estate of William Gaston, dec. August term, 1837.
No names given. (RD) August 8, 1837. (CLK) Harrison Glas-

cock.

46) Final settlement of Philip O. West, adm. of the estate of Absalom Carlisle. August term. 1837.
No names given. (RD) August 8, 1837, (CLK) Harrison Glascock.

47) Settlement of Dabney Jones and Frances Conn, adm. of the estate James Ledford, dec. August term, 1837.
Monies Expended: D. Jones, F. Conn, Charles Glascock. (RD) August 9, 1837, (CLK) Harrison Glascock.

48) Final settlement of James Glascock, exr. of the estate of Noah Glascock, dec. August term, 1837.
Monies Received: Jacob Fry, agent for Isac Fry; J.C. Ferguson, James C. Barnett, Benj. Stinson, Hiram Glascock, A. Clarlisle.
Monies Expended: Lucy J. Glascock, guardian for Lucy Glascock. (RD) August 9, 1837, (CLK) Harrison Glascock.

49) Settlement of Dabney Jones, adm. of the estate of Benjn. Benn, dec. August term, 1837.
No names given. (RD) August 14, 1837, (CLK) Harrison Glascock.

50) Settlement of Dabney Jones, adm. of the estate of Patrick M. Glenn, dec. August term, 1837.
Monies Received: Jessee Hildreth, Richard Nicholds, Asa Fowler, Wm. Jones, Nathan Mefford, Benson Whitledge, Samuel Gillespie, Dabney Jones.
Monies Expended: J. Stark, Heath Jones, Stephen Cleaver, I. Lewellen, James Carson, William Young. (RD) August 14, 1837, (CLK) Harrison Glascock.

51) Annual settlement of Mary Krigbaum, etrx. of Jacob Krigbaum, dec.
No names given. (RD) August 14, 1837, (CLK) H. Glascock.

52) Luke W. Watkins, adm. of the estate of Hillson Griffin made final settlement. August, 1837.
No names given. (RD) August 15, 1837, (CLK) Harrison Glascock.

53) Annual settlement of Jeptha Crosthwaite, adm. of the estate of John F. Elliott. November term, 1837.
Monies Received: P. W. Pierce, Ballis (sic) M'Pherson.
Monies Expended: Widow Elliott, R. King, Wm. O. Young. (RD) November 6, 1837, (CLK) Harrison Glascock.

54) Final settlement of Harrison Glascock, adm. of Nimrod Glasock, dec. November term, 1837.
Monies Received: John Glascock.
Money expended: R. King, C. Carstarphen, C. Glascock, R. H. M'Kay, Wm. Carson, A.B. Chambers. (RD) November 6, 1837, (CLK) Harrison Glascock.

55) Annual settlement of Jonathan Barnard, adm. of the estate of Jonathan Barnard. November term, 1837.
Monies Received: J. S. Ely, J. Stewart, Jas. Underwood,

7

Wm. Gatson, J. Gatson, J. Ely. (RD) November 6, 1837, (CLK)
Harrison Glascock.
56) Final settlement of John M. Johnson, adm. of John R.
Dykes, dec., November term, 1837.
Monies Expended: Daniel Kendrick, Wm. Carson, H. Glascock
(RD) November 7, 1837, (CLK) Harrison Glascock.
57) Annual settlement of Cassy Grant, adx. of the estate
of Peter Grant, dec. November term, 1837.
No names given. (RD) November 7, 1837, (CLK) Harrison
Glascock.
58) Settlement of Wm. Priest, exr. of John Payne, dec.
No names given. (RD) November 8, 1837, (CLK) Harrison
Glascock.
59) Settlement of Luke W. Watkins, adm. of William S.
Gaunt, dec.
Monies Received: William K. Flowerree (sic), John Tracy,
Robert B. Caldwell, O. H. P. Markle, Parker Dimmitt, John J.
Slosson, Squire Brothers, Samuel K. Caldwell,Abraham Buford,
N. T. Pierce, Samuel H. Hill, Joseph G. Aldridge, A.K. Fike,
Bartlet White, John Jamison, John D. Tucker, Daniel Brown,
Nancy Ledford, Oney Carstarphen, Drury Edes, Joseph Fanning.
Monies Expended: A. & W. M. Merby, Dabney Jones, George
Sterret, James L. Fisher, Russel King, Joseph D. Tapley, J.
C. Hays, William G. Johnson. (RD) November 8, 1837, (CLK)
Harrison Glascock.
60) John Jamsion and Andromicha, adm. of the estate of
William Jamison, dec. make their final settlement.
Monies Received: John Tracy, John D. White, Wm. Jenkins,
Saml. H. Hill, Stephen Glascock, John Jamison, Andromacha
Jamison, Sydney Fisher, G. S. Fisher, Simon Davis, Samuel W.
Mayhall, Chas. Glascock.
Monies Eexpended: John Tracy, Lewis Tracy, John D. White,
Abraham Buford, Saml. H. Hill, John D. White, J.J. Slosson,
Oney Carstarphen, Luke W. Watkins, J. & J. N. Griffin, John
Jamison, George C. Hays, A. Elgins. (RD) November 8, 1837,
(CLK) Harrison Glascock.
61) Walter Caldwell, adm. of the estate of William Jack-
son files his annual settlement. November term, 1837.
Monies Eexpended: Joshua Bosley, Wm. Peake, Lewis Tracy,
George C. Hays, Samuel K. Caldwell. (RD) November 24, 1837,
(RD) Harrison Glascock.
62) Annual settlement of Maria Dodd, admx. of Stephen
Dod, dec. February term, 1838.
Monies Received: James Rackliff, French Glascock, adm. of
A. Jefferies, Hiram Glascock, Charles Glascock, Turner G.
Priest, John B. Dodd, Joseph D. Gash, William Brown, David
D. Dumlap, Allen Dodd, Louis Dodd.
Monies Expended: Margaret M. Baris, Charles Glascock,
Allen Dodd. (RD) February 5, 1838, (CLK) Harrison Glascock.

63) Settlement of James and Robert McGee, adm. of the estate of John McGee, dec. November term, 1837. Monies Expended: E. McBride, Charles Glascock, W. Caldwell, George Glenn, W. K. Vanasall, H. Glascock. (RD) February 6, 1838, (CLK) Harrison Glascock.

64) Annual settlement of Elijah Hudson, adm. of the estate of William Hudson, dec. February term, 1838. Monies Expended: Willi S. Lofland, D. Jones, S. Cleaver. (RD) February 6, 1838, (CLK) Harrison Glascock.

65) Annual settlement of Kemp M. Glascock, adm. of Ann M. Glascock, dec. February term, 1838. No names given. (RD) February 6, 1838, (CLK) Harrison Glascock.

66) Annual settlement of John Briscoe, adm. of the estate of Ralph D. Briscoe, dec. February term, 1838. No names given. (RD) February 7, 1838, (CLK) Harrison Glascock.

67) Annual settlement of William Rodgers, adm. of H. Rogers, dec. February term, 1837. No names given. (RD) February 7, 1838, (CLK) Harrison Glascock.

68) Final settlement of Kemp M. Glascock, adm. of the estate of Ann M. Glascock. May term, 1838. No names given. (RD) May 7, 1838, (CLK) Harrison Glascock

69) Annual settlement of Elizabeth Jefferies, admx. of the estate of Robert Jefferies, dec. May term, 1838. Monies Expended: White Cotten, --- Clayton, L. Tracy, J. Croswaite, --- McMurty, G. Clayton, H. Glascock, --- Purdom, Chambers & Harris, John Conn, Robt. Hays. (RD) May 8, 1838, (CLK) Harrison Glascock.

70) Annual settlement of Philip Field, adm. of the estate of John Field, dec. May term, 1838. Monies Received: Chapel Carstarpehen, -- Barkley, William Brown, L. W. Watkins, Mayhall & Slossin (RD) May 8, 1838, (CLK) Harrison Glascock.

71) Annual settlement of Dr. George Settle, adm. of the estate of Tetrarch Fall, dec. May term, 1838. Monies Received: John W. Spencer, M. J. Noyes. Monies Expended: J. M. Calhoun, Cambrick & Stockings, Wm. Greathouse, J. Lyle, Chambers & Harris, Harrison Hawkins, of Pike County. (RD) June 11, 1838, (CLK) Harrison Glascock.

72) Final settlement of Jonathan Abbey, sr., adm. of the estate of George B. Abbey, dec. August term, 1837. No names given. (RD) May 31, 1839, (CLK) John Ralls, Filed August 8, 1838.

73) Annual settlement of Mathew Elliott, exr. of the estate of Stephen Elliott, dec. August term, 1838. Monies Expended: On February 20, 1838 paid John I. Lyle on account for self to Deborah Lyle and Martin Lyle. On

February 22, 1838 paid John Elliott on note for Wm. Harger. Mentioned are: John Elliott, Myers Mobley, Richard Matson, Jesse Boarman, James Brant. (RD) May 31, 1839, (CLK) John Ralls, (FD) August 13, 1838.

74) Settlement of William W. Cartmill, adm. of the estate of John Crockett, dec. May term, 1838.

Monies Received: Sale of personal property of the deceased on March 4, 1837. Mentioned: William Power and David Ingram.

Monies Expended: E.A. Swiney, M. Walton, Matthew Elliott, Wilkerson & Tally, William Liney, Jonathan Abbey, Joseph Hopson, Philip Myers. (RD) May 31, 1839, (CLK) John Ralls, Filed August 31, 1838.

75) Annual settlement of Joshua Ely, adm. of the estate of Thomas Ely, dec.

No names given. (RD) May 31, 1839, (CLK) John Ralls, Filed August 13, 1838.

76) Annual settlement of Johnson Bernard adm. of the estate of Peter Grant, dec. November term, 1838.

No names given. (RD) May 31, 1839, (CLK) John Ralls, Filed November 6, 1838.

77) Final settlement by Richd. Boyce, adm. of the estate of Silsbury C. Garnet, dec.

Monies Received: A judgement was obtained by R. B. Bartlett, former administrator at the August term, 1834, of the Supreme Court, against Edmund Hyde.

Monies Expended: Uirel Wright, -- Chambers, H. Glascock. (RD) May 31, 1839, (CLK) John Ralls, (FD) November 6, 1838.

78) Settlement by John Briscoe, adm. of the estate of of Ralph D. Briscoe, dec. November term, 1838.

No names given. (RD) May 31, 1839, (CLK) John Ralls, Filed November 6, 1838.

79) Final settlement of Elizabeth Jefferies, admx. of the estate of Robert Jefferies, dec. November term, 1838.

Monies Expended: H. Chitwood, -- Fike, J. Croswaithe, Dr. Caldwell. (RD) May 31, 1839, (CLK) John Ralls, (FD) November 6, 1838.

80) Annual settlement of Johnson Bernard, exr. of the estate of Jonathan Bernard, dec. November term, 1838.

Monies Expended: Rueben Reddish, Henry Fagan. (RD) May 31, 1839, (CLK) John Ralls, (FD) November 6, 1838.

81) Settlement of William Priest, exr. of the estate of John Payne, dec.

No names given. (RD) May 31, 1839, (CLK) John Ralls, Filed November 5, 1838.

82) Annual settlement by Tho. M. Campbell, exr. of James Campbell, dec. November term, 1838.

Monies Received: B. W. Halls, J. W. Orear Apperson & Chiles.

Monies Expended: Shaw & Heller, Hesket & Darnes, Robert Allison. Expenses by the executor to and from Kentucky. (RD) May 31, 1839, (CLK) John Ralls, (FD) December 3, 1838.

83) Second annual settlement of Mariah Dodd, admx. of Stephen Dodd, dec. February term, 1839.
Monies Received: Eli C. Gallaher, Wm. Carver. (RD) May 31, 1839, (CLK) John Ralls, (FD) February 4, 1839.

84) Annual settlement of Geo. L. Hardy and Joseph A. Hardy, adm. of Arnold Hardy, dec.
Monies Received: James Alexander, Geo. L. Hardy. (RD) May 31, 1839, (CLK) John Ralls, (FD) February 4, 1839.

85) Settlement of James Inlow, adm. of Peyton P. Wright, dec. February term, 1839.
Monies Expended: G. C. Hays, Pearce & Wright, A. and W. McMurty, G. Clayton, Joseph Fanning, Mahall & Slosson. (RD) May 31, 1839, (CLK) John Ralls, Filed February 4, 1839.

86) Annual Settlement of Dabney Jones, adm, of the estate of Patrick M. Glenn, dec. October term, 1838.
Monies Expended: Ezekiel Ferrel, William Moss, John W. Williams, Joseph Fanning. (RD) June 1, 1839, (CLK) John Ralls, (FD) February 5, 1839.

87) Annual settlement of Elijah Hudson, adm. of the estate of William Hudson, dec. February term, 1839.
Monies Expended: John P. Turner, Vermillion. (RD) June 1, 1839, (CLK) John Ralls, (FD) February 26, 1839.

88) Annual settlement of William Rodgers, adm. of the estate of Hamilton Rodgers, dec. February term, 1839.
No names given. (RD) June 1, 1839, (CLK) John Ralls, (FD) February 25, 1839.

89) Annual settlement of -- Field, adm. of the estate of John Field, dec. May term, 1839.
No names given. (RD) June 1, 1839, (CLK) John Ralls, (FD) May 6, 1839.

90) Annual settlement of George Settle, adm. of the estate of Tetrach Fall, dec. May term, 1839.
Monies Received: Thos. Brashear, Joel Finks, John W. Spencer.
Monies Expended: Mary McLeland, John McCune, Allen Rouse, Nicholas Rouse, James Bryant, B. F. Hawkins. (RD) June 1, 1839, (CLK) John Ralls, (FD) May 6, 1839.

91) Final settlement of Maria Dodd, admx. of the estate of Stephen Dodd, dec. May term, 1839.
Monies Received: Griffith D. Shellton, David O. Glascock, Charles Glascock, Marcus Hall.
Monies Expended: Uriel Wright, Dav. O. and Charles Glascock, Harrison Glascock, John Ralls. (RD) June 1, 1839, (CLK) John Ralls, (FD) May 7, 1839.

92) Third annual settlement of Matthew Elliot, exr. of the estate of Stephen Elliott, dec.

Monies Received: Raymond Elliott.

Monies Expended: David Blue, Dr. Jas. D. Caldwell, Jeptha Boarman, Michael Blue. (RD) June 10, 1839, (CLK) John Ralls.

93) Final settlement by Luke W. Watkins & Noah O. Gant, adm. of the estate of William S. Gant, dec. May term, 1839.

Monies Received: Rent of house in 1839 to Wm. G. Johnson. Rent in 1937 for grocery from Samuel Mayhall. Rent for stable from Joseph E. Gatewood in 1837. Rent for grocery from James W. Hawkins in 1838. Rent for dwelling house from J. Tracy in 1838. Rent of house due November 28, 1839 for Lewis Tracy in 1839. Account collections from: John Ross, J. L.(?) Croswaite, William Thompson, Alexr. Buford, Robert Jeffery, Thomas L. Barkley, Robert Welldie, Hugh A. Barkley, Hanceford Brawn, Adam Bast, William G. Johnson, Joshua Ely, Stephen Glascock, Robert Dillard, John Hawkins, Joshua T. Hope, Edward Mattox, Daniel R. Ledford, Benjamin Levers, Harvey McGawin, William Hays, Jefferson Hays,Westley Seabee, George Haverback, Absalem Fears, Joseph Wright, Joseph Rice, John Layne, Daniel Herrin, Thomas Bauls, Mathew Smith, James Emesan, jr., Joel Ledford, Robert Tritkier, Richard Boarman, William Treadway, William D. Barkley, James Chitwood, Jacob Krigbaum, Charles Bohnan, William Bayds, Larkin G. Field, William Kregbaum, John Doaly, John Ely, William Moss, Thomas S. Johnson, Aaron Fagan, Moses Richardson, jr., John Chitwood, James C. Barnet.

Monies Expended: David R. Willson, Lewis Tracy, George Waller, Hosea Northcutt, Henry P. Smith, Daniel Brown, James Emerson, Joseph Fanning, Christopher Rhodes, James C. Barnet. (RD) June 10, 1839, (CLK) John Ralls.

94) Final settlement by Joshua I. Ely, adm. of the estate of Thomas Ely, dec.

Monies Received: Thomas Brashears, I. Huston, Robert E. Spotswood, Jesse E. Richardson, Bennett Gardner, Jacob B. Shibley.

Monies Expended: C. Carstarphen, Jesse Boarman, John Coleman, G. L. Hardy, Hays & Gove, B. F. Hayden.

Notes due: --- Rice, L. W. Mayhall, Margaret Ely, John Howard, Joseph Hardy, Thomas G. Gardner, Joshua Ely.

Note: (Apparently there has been a change in the administrator for the estate. The new administrator is Benjamin Ely. He states that the above information was received from Joshua Ely on August 6, 1839) (RD) August 5,1839, (CLK) J. Ralls.

95) Final settlement by Jeptha I. Croswaite, adm. of the estate of John F. Elliott, dec. August term, 1839.

Monies Received: Richard Matson, Bartlett White, H. Brown, John Briscoe, J. S. Croswaite, Joseph Wright, John Field, T. S. Barkley.

Monies Expended: -- Matson, John Briscoe, J.S. Croswaite, Joseph Wright, Joel Ledford. (RD) August 5, 1839, (CLK) John

Ralls.

96) Final settlement of Mary Krigbaum, admx. of Jacob Krigbaum, sr., dec. August term, 1839.
Monies Expended: --- Noyes. (RD) August 6, 1839, (CLK) John Ralls.

97) Final settlement of John Gaston, adm. of the estate of William Gaston, dec. August term, 1839.
Monies Expended: J. Boarman, J. J. Lyle, H. Watson, L. Dooley, McGruder & Henderson, J. Fegan, Johnson Bernard, Joseph Biggibs, Smith Gatson, H. Glascock, (RD) August 6, 1839, (CLK) John Ralls.

98) Annual settlement of William W. Cartwell, adm. of the estate of John Crockett, dec. August term, 1839.
Monies Expended: H. Glascock, John A. Quals, John Gatson, J. Abey, James Crocket, Robert Crocket, mention of a suit in Kentucky. (RD) August 6, 1839, (CLK) John Ralls.

99) Final settlement by Daniel Hendricks, adm. of the estate of Samuel Conway, dec. September term, 1839.
No names given. (RD) September 10, 1839, (CLK) J. Ralls.

100) Final settlement by Walter Caldwell, adm. of the estate of William J. Jackson. September term, 1839.
No names givens. (RD) September 10, 1839, (CLK) J. Ralls

101) Final settlement of Johnson Barnard, exr. of the estate of Jonathan Barnard, dec. November term, 1839.
Money received: Thos. Dooly, Johnson Barnard, Rueben Readish, Henry Wolfe, H. Fagan, Wm. Carter, Wm. Sinclear, James Roland.
Money expended: Wm. Carter, --- Sinclear, J. Roland, Matthew Elliott. (RD) November 6, 1839, (CLK) John Ralls.

102) Annual settlement by Johnson Barnard, adm. of the estate of Peter Grant, dec. November term, 1839.
No names given. (RD) November 5, 1839, (CLK) John Ralls.

103) Accounting of William Priest, adm. of the estate of John Payne, dec. November term, 1839.
Negro girl, Maria, delivered to Daniel Payne on May 16, 1839. (RD) November 5, 1839, (CLK) John Ralls.

104) Settlement of Gabriel Penn, adm. of Horatio Penn, dec. November term, 1839.
Monies Expended: Elijah N. Hascall, James Shohoney. (RD) November 4, 1839, (CLK) John Ralls.

105) Settlement by Thomas Campbell, adm. of the estate of James Campbell, dec. November term, 1839.
Monies Expended: John R. Carter, John W. Ragsdale, James Underwood, Johnson Barnard, R. H. Buchanan, Landi Fagan, W. R. Campbell, Meredith & Thomas, Reuben Reddish, Thomas M. Campbell. (RD) November 4, 1839, (CLK) John Ralls.

106) Settlement of Benjamin Ely, adm. of the estate of Thomas Ely, dec. December term, 1839.
No names given. (RD) December 11, 1839, (CLK) John Ralls.

107) Settlement of Joseph Fanning, adm. of the estate of Middleton Fanning, dec. February term, 1840.
Notes due August 4, 1839 and not yet collected: Margaret Hilton, John Rinny, Jacob Fudge, J. Calhourn.
Notes on Account: Sary Lee, James Fanning.
Credits: Wm. Leek.
Expenditures: John Lyle, - Rice, - Carstaphen, - Pierce. (RD) February 5, 1840, (CLK) John Ralls.
108) Settlement of James Inlow, adm. of the estate of Paton P. Wright. February term, 1840.
Monies Received: I. Wright, Joel Ledford, H. Inlow, Wm. Inlow, Eaton Turner, W. Johnston (note due on December 25, 1840).
Monies Expended: John A. Wright, guard. of infant heirs of P. P. Wright; Lewis Tracy; Dr. McCay; Joseph Wright; H. Brown; D. Jones; Shields & Emerson; P. Pierce; Henry Inlow; Joseph and Sanford. (RD) February 3, 1840, (CLK) John Ralls.
109) Annual Settlement by John H. Lynch and Matthew Elliott, exrs., of the the estate of Bernard I. Lynch. February term, 1840.
Monies Received: Sale of personal property on November 23, 1838.
Monies Expended - Name/Date: Jas. T. I. McElroy, June 13, 1840; Hays & Gore (funeral expenses), August 14, 1839; Ortha Brashears (for crying), July 18, 1839; Hays & Gore, August 14, 1840; L. W. Watkins, June 13, 1840; Cornelius N. Lynch, February 1, 1840; J. J. Lyle, February 1, 1840; Luke W. Watkins (for counsel), February 5, 1840; C. Carstarphen, June 8, 1839; John M. Byars; Chars. M. Asher for William L. Lynch. (RD) February 3, 1840; (CLK) John Ralls.
110) Annual Settlement of Robert Moss, adm. of the estate of Joseph C. Epperson. February term, 1840.
Monies Received: Joseph Hardy (for rent of land); sale of negro man, Darrell, to Joseph Wright on January 1, 1840. (RD) February 4, 1840, (CLK) John Ralls.
111) William Rogers, adm. of the estate of Hamilton Rogers, dec. made an annual settlement. February term, 1840.
No names given. (RD) February 4, 1840, (CLK) John Ralls.
112) Dabney Jones, adm. of the estate of P. M. Glenn, dec. made an annual settlement. February term, 1840.
No names given. (RD) February 4, 1840, (CLK) John Ralls.
113) Annual settlement of the estate of John Dorshimer, dec., by William Sox, jr., adm. February term, 1840.
Monies Received: Acy Glascock, --- Culbertson, John Ely, William Jameson, J. Krigbaum.

14

Monies Expended: William Tracy. (RD) February 5, 1850, (CLK) John Ralls.

114) Annual settlement of Lewis S. Anderson, adm. of the estate of John H. Anderson, dec. February adjourned term, 1840, on March 16, 1840.

Monies Received: Widow mentioned, but no name given.

Monies Expended: Hays & Gore, Widow, Mrs. Anderson, mentioned. (RD) March 16, 1840, (CLK) John Ralls.

115) Final settlement of the estate of Stephen Elliott, dec. by Matthew Elliott, exr. May term, 1840.

No names given. (RD) May 18, 1840, (CLK) John Ralls.

116) Final settlement of the estate of John Field, dec. by Phillip F. Field, adm. May term, 1840.

Monies Expended: H. Glascock, Jno. Ralls. (RD) May 18, 1840, (CLK) John Ralls.

117) Annual settlement of William W. Cartwill, adm. of the estate of John Crocket, dec. May term, 1840.

Monies Received: Hire of negro girl to Johnson Barmard; Hire of negro boy to Andrew McElroy; Rent of place for 1839 from G. Leney, Sale of negro girl to James Fagan. (RD) May 19, 1840, (CLK) John Ralls.

118) Annual settlement of Benjamin Ely, adm. of the estate of Thomas Ely, dec. August term, 1840.

Monies Expended: Margaret Ely, Joshua Ely, Benjn. Ely, S. and M. Boyd. (RD) August 5, 1840, (CLK) John Ralls.

119) First annual settlement of Joel Finks, adm. of the estate of Robert Jones, dec. August term, 1840.

Monies Expended: Joshua Wilson, C. T. Taylor, Matthew Elliott. (RD) August 3, 1840, (CLK) John Ralls.

120) Annual settlement of Elizabeth Wilson, adm. of the estate of Presly Wilson. August term, 1840.

Monies Received: Receipt on J. J. Slosson for a note on J. Fanning and Jonah Jackson, note on Levy N. Bolvar, note on George L. Hardy, note on Aron Blakeman. Sale bill was made on July 12, 1839.

Monies Expended: David Thomas, B. F. Haden, L. Anderson, J. J. Slosson, Jacob Fuqua, J. F. Hawkins, John F. Austin, Hays & Gore, N. T. Pierce, W. P. Torrance, --- Haden, Benj. Ely, Joseph Fanning. (RD) August 5, 1840, (CLK) John Ralls.

121) Final settlement of Johnson Barnard, adm. of the estate of Peter Grant, dec. August term, 1840.

Monies Received: Joseph Biggers (sale of land); -- Buckhannon.

Monies Expended: Cissell & Roberts, Magruder & Handon, -- Chawming, Byant & son, Bryant & Payne, Meredith & Thomas, Robert Haines, Enoch Fruit, Robert Hanna, John Rlls, L. F. Hall, G. C. Hays, Mrs. Grant. (RD) September 14, 1840 (CLK) John Ralls.

122) Annual settlement of William W. Cartwill, adm. of

15

the estate of John Crocket, dec. August term, 1840.
Monies Received: Robert Crocket, John Crocket of Kentucky, --- Underwood, George Linney, William Martin.
Monies Expended: Elijah Crocket, James Crocket, Jackson Crocket, Eli Crocket, Carlile Crocket, Robert Crocket, William Linney, Julian Nucum, J. Barnard, M.J. Noyce, J. Ralls, Wm. Martin. (RD) September 16, 1840, (CLK) John Ralls.

123) Final settlement of Thomas Campbell, exr. of the estate of James Campbell, dec. November term, 1840.
Monies Expended: Apperson & Chile, James D. Caldwell, W. N. Penn, John Scobee, Johnathan Abbay, sr., Thomas M. Campbell, H. Glascock, J. Abbay, J. Ralls. (RD) November 2, 1840, (CLK) John Ralls.

124) Final settlement of John H. Lynch and Matthew Elliott, exrs. of the estate of Bernard I. Lynch. November term, 1840.
Monies Received: Daniel B. Kendrick, John Blue.
Monies Expended: John H. Lynch, Speed Ely, Isaac Ely, George C. Hays, A. H. Buckner, Andrew McElroy, B. W. Brown, George W. Patee, Cornelius N. Lynch, Chars. Glascock, Robt. Steward, John Ralls, Matthew Elliott, --- Noyes, William L. Lynch, Elisha Lynch, James Fagan. (RD) November 4, 1840, (CLK) John Ralls.

125) Settlement of Gabriel Penn, adm. of Horatio Penn. December term, 1840.
Monies Expended: S. W. Mayhall, --- Eastman, Joseph F. Abbington. (RD) December 14, 1840, (CLK) John Ralls.

126) First annual settlement of French Glascock, adm. of the estate of Charles Glascock, dec. November adjourned term, 1840.
Monies Received: Note of Jas. Neal for 1445-1/2 gal. of whiskey that was sold to -- Choteau in St. Louis, bill against the heirs of R. Brewer, 533-1/3 gal. of whiskey sold to B. Markle, 63-1/2 gal. sold to John Bates, 47-3/4 bush. of rye sold to B. Settle, John M. Johnson for rent, payment in full by Aaron Gernsay for his note, payment in full by W. Moss for his note, Johnson Saunders account with the estate, Wm. Graham, Samuel Newland, Samuel Smith, Jos. Rice, Joseph Canaway, Harris Hopkins, Wm. S. Sims, T. F. Offett. (RD) December 44, 1840, (CLK) John Ralls.

127) Final settlement of Elijah Hudson, adm. of the estate of William Hudson, dec. November term, 1840.
Monies Received: Land bought by David Brothers, Achilas McGinas.
Monies Expended: Heirs of Nimrod Triplitt, Daniel F. J. Browning, Pleasant Hudson, John P. Turner, Thomas Cleaver, James Hudson, David Shepard, Peter D. Moyer, Aaron Figgins, David Brothers, Achilles McGinnis, W. S. Lofland, H. Glascock. (RD) December 15, 1840, (CLK) John Ralls.

128)   James D. Watson, exr. of the will of John Watson, dec.

Monies Expended: William L. Sergeant, Shilton Watson, William Watson, John Brockman, Joseph Polson, Shelton (sic) Watson. (RD) February 1, 1841, (CLK) John Ralls.

129) Annual settlement of Neal Camron, adm. of the estate of Joshua Rlls, dec. February term, 1841.

Monies Received: Note dated April 1, 1839 by Thomas H. Griffith. S. B. Pavilion paid wages on May 11, 1840. S. D. Philpes note dated March 31, 1839. Cash received of Thomas H. Griffith for the one sixteenth part of S. D. Pavilion sold to him on February 25, 1840 and to be paid on December 17th.   (RD) February 1, 1841, (CLK) John Ralls.

130) Final settlement by James Inlow, adm. of the estate of Peyton P. Wright, dec. February term, 1841.

John A. Wright was mentioned with a guardian receipt. (RD) February 2, 1841, (CLK) John Ralls.

131) First annual settlement of Rebecca Haines, adm. of the estate of Jesse Haines, dec. February term, 1841.

Monies Received: $763 on hand in July, 1835.

Monies Expended: Boarding of Mary Anders from July 4, 1835 to November 12, 1840. Boarding of Nancy and Martha Haines from July 4, 1835 to February 2, 1841. (RD) February 2, 1841, (CLK) John Haines.

132) Annual of Robert Moss, adm. of the estate of --- Epperson, dec. February term, 1841.

Monies Expended: J. S. Crosthwait, Abner Smith, Gilmore S. Morehead, --- Ely, William McCune (assignee of Posey N. Smith), Bernard Rice, Robert Moss, E. G. McGrea, Samuel D. Rice, Wm. H. Peake, Wm. McCune, Joseph Wright, Dabney Jones, Elizabeth Jefferies, John N. Daniel, P. N. Smith, Emerson & Shields, Robert Dillard, Isaac Lettr (sic), Hosey Northcutt, Campbell & Chiton, J. S. Crosthwait. (RD) February 2, 1841, (CLK) John Ralls.

133) Settlement of Philip Field, adm. of John Field, dec. February term, 1841.

Money Expended: J. Hornback, John D. Field, Mary Field, Silas Field. (RD) February 13, 1841, (CLK) John Ralls.

134) First annual settlement of James Culbertson and Wm. H. Vardeman, adms. of the estate of Richard Matson, dec. February term, 1841.

Monies Received: Uriel Wright's receipt for a note on P. A. Labeaume dated May 5, 1837. One note on James L. Fisher and C. Rice dated March 5, 1838 and due September 15, 1839. One note on James L. Fisher and C. Rice dated March 5, 1838 and due September 15, 1840. One note on Charles Rice dated February 19, 1833 and due seven years later. Monies received from Rueben D. H. Low, James L. Fisher, Joseph Hardy and A. S. Saul. One note on A. McGinnis assigned by J. A. Boarman dated November, 1829 and with a credit of $2.37 on October 25, 1850. Interest on Hosea Northcutt's note. One note on A. S. Saul and Simon Davis dated July 7, 1840 and due December 25, 1840. Money received from James L. Fisher for the hire of Washington (sic) from November 15, 1838 to September 15, 1839. Money received from a note on Thomas and Jessy Lear. One note on James L. Fisher and Simon Davis dated September 14, 1840 and due a year later. One note on Thomas and Jesse (sic) Lear dated January 22, 1841. Money received from James L. Fisher for the hire of Washington from September 15, 1839 to 1840. Monies received from Thomas and Jesse Lear, James Culbertson and James L. Fisher.

Monies Expended: January 1st - cash paid to --- Garick for a cap for Wash. January 1st - cash paid to --- Eastman for boots for Wash. December 30, 1839 to J. Lasey, February 4, 1840 to James L. Fisher, February 4, 1840 to J. B. Vardeman, August 5, 1850 to James L. Fisher, August 14, 1840 J. Sosey, September 14, 1840 to James L. Fisher, November 1, 1840 to N. Pierce and D. Wilcox, November 3, 1840 to George Fisher, money paid for taxes on land in Marion County, December 3, 1841 to A. S. Saul, January 27, 1841 to G.C. Hays and Joseph Hardy, January 22, 1841 to Thomas Lear, Jesse Lear and James Culbertson. (RD) February 13, 1841, (CLK) John Ralls.

135)   Annual settlement of James McGee, exr. of the estate of James Lee, dec. February term, 1841.

Monies Recieved: James T. McElroy, Thos. L. Anderson, William Muldron.

Monies Expended: --- Steward, --- Hardy, D. Rice, Hays & Gore, Dr. McElroy and to the Widow. (RD) March 22, 1841, (CLK) John Ralls.

136)   First annual settlement of Daniel B. Kendrick and Guilford D. Hansboroguh, adms. of the estate of Harvey Wilson, dec. May term, 1841.

Monies received: Sale Bill on July 25, 1841. (sic)

Monies Expended: Tax receipts paid for 1839 and 1840. Evan Antwerp for tuition, George L. Hardy, Narciccus Wilson's receipt for a note on James Donelson, Dallis & Able, Hays & Gore, the Widow. (RD) May 3, 1841. (CLK) John Ralls.

137)   First annual settlement by James G. Wylie and Peasant Cox, adms. of the estate of William Wylie, dec. May term, 1841.

Monies Expended: February 25, 1841 to Isaac L. Holt, April 23, 1840 to T. B. Stevens, April 25, 1840 to I. S. Buchannon, March 1, 1841 to Russel King, May 3, 1841 to N. Pierc, April 7, 1840 to I. Paterson for clothing for a black woman, and monies paid to Pleasant Cox, J. G. Wylie and J. C. Wilbern. (RD) May 3, 1841, (CLK) John Ralls.

138)   Annual settlement of John and George Billings, exr.

of the estate of Abraham Billings, dec. May term, 1841.
Monies Received: One note on Harvey Wellman due January,
1840. One note on Harvey Wellman due January 1, 1841. One
note on J. A. Francis and due on December 25, 1838, and
notes on E. N. Hicall and S. C. Haldebeck.
Monies Expended: January 25, 1840 to John Akin, January,
1841 to James Hampton, January, 1841 to Margaret Carson,
February, 1840 to John Akin, October, 1840 to Joh Akin,
February, 1840 to E. N. Hiscal and F. Hiscal. (RD) May 3,
1841, (CLK) John Ralls.
139) Final settlement of William Rodgers, adm. of the
estate of Hamilton Rogers, dec. May term, 1841.
Monies Received: Money on hand as of February, 1838.
Monies Expended: May 3, 1841 to Joseph Rogers, May 3,
1841 to Lorinda R. Rogers, H. Glascock, J. Ralls. (RD) May
4, 1841, (CLK) John Ralls.
140) First annual settlement of Richard Bolware, adm. of
the estate of Logan Bolware, dec. May term, 1841.
Money Expended: Widow mentioned. John Blue, John Straer.
(RD) May 4, 1841, (CLK) John Ralls.
141) First annual settlement of C. Carstarphen, adm. of
the estate of Wm. R. Brown, dec. May adjourned term, 1841.
Monies Expended: January 5th to James D. Caldwell, A. B.
Combs. (RD) June 4, 1841, (CLK) John Ralls.
142) Annual settlement of Rapheal Leake, adm. of the
estate of John Gillespie, dec. June term, 1841.
Monies Expended: June 7, 1841 to J. Piereall. (RD) June
7, 1841, (CLK) John Ralls.
143) Settlement of Peggy Davis, extrix. of the will of
Robert Davis, dec. June term, 1841.
Heirs: Malinda Davis now named Malinda Hyde, Robert Montgomery Davis, Catharine Davis, Adaline Davis.
Extrx. Signature: Margaret M. Davis. (RD) June 8, 1841,
(CLK) John Ralls.
144) Final Settlement of Lewis S. Anderson, adm. of the
estate of John H. Anderson, dec. May term, 1841.
Monies Expended: Dr. Lyle, Lewis Anderson, Elizabeth Anderson, Martha Anderson, Nancy Anderson, James Anderson,
John H. Anderson. (RD) June 8, 1841, (CLK) John Ralls.
145) Annual settlement by Benjamin Ely, adm. of the estate Thomas Ely, dec. August term, 1841.
Monies Received: Monies due on August 5, 1840 to the guardian of Benjamin Ely, James Ely and Thomas Ely.
Monies Expended: Tax collector's receipt for 1839 and
1840, Sarah Lee and John Ralls. (RD) August 3, 1841, (CLK)
John Ralls.
146) Settlement by James D. Watson, exr. for the estate
of John Watson, dec. August term, 1841.
Monies Expended: Trips by the executor to Virginia and

Tennessee. (RD) August 3, 1841, (CLK) John Ralls.
147) Annual settlement of Elizabeth Wilson, adm. of the estate of Presley Wilson, dec. September term, 1841. Monies Expended: J. Culbert, Joseph M. Hampton, Hays & Gore, Extr. of the estate of Harvey Wilson, dec., William Wilson as one of the heirs, Elizabeth Wilson. (RD) September 13, 1841, (CLK) John Ralls.
148) First annual settlement by Abraham Buford, jr., adm. of the estate of John Buford, dec. September term, 1841. Monies Received: October 5, 1840 sale bill date. Monies Expended: August, 1840 to J. D. Buchanon, August 30, 1840 to --- McMurty for shoes, August, 21, 1840 to --- Tracy for coffin, John Ralls. (RD) September 13, 1840, (CLK) John Ralls.
149) Settlement of Eliza Offut (sic), adm. of the estate of Thornton F. Offutt, dec. September term, 1841. Monies Received: Inventory of estate September, 1841. Monies Expended: September, 1841 to Stephen Smith for funeral expenses, M. Floweree, V. P. Demmitt, Mrs. Parker, D. Bowling. (RD) September 13, 1841, (CLK) John Ralls.
150) First annual settlement of James Epperson, adm. of the estate of Joel Taylor, dec. September term, 1841. Monies Received: Judgement against John V. Mills on October 24, 1840. (RD) September 13, 1840, (CLK) John Ralls.
151) First annual settlement of Stephen E. Elliott, adm. of the estate of John Elliott, dec. August term, 1841. Monies Expended: John M. Colhourne for coffin, J. B. Gore for funeral, J. L. Lyle, physician. (RD) September 13, 1841, (CLK) John Ralls.
152) First annual settlement by Stephen McPherson, adm. of the estate of Eli C. Galleher, dec. September term, 1841. Monies Received: Hire of Isaac, a black man. Sale bill dated August 12, 1840. Sale of land mentioned. Monies received from Stephen McPherson and Thomas F. Offutt. Monies Expended: Floweree & Menifee, Stephen Smith, Wm. O. Lofland, Samuel Ely, Samuel Smith, S. W. Mayhall, A. W. McMurty, Uirel Wright, N. T. Pierce, --- Buckhannon, John Glascock, Stephen Cleaver, Stephen McPherson, Mrs. Bahanan. (RD) September 14, 1841, (CLK) John Ralls.
153) First annual settlement of Abraham Selly, adm. of the estate of Nelly Johnston, dec. November term, 1841. Monies Received: Cash from the estate of John N. Seely, dec. for the use said Nelly Johnston, dec. (RD) November 1, 1841, (CLK) John Ralls.
154) First annual settlement of Otho Brashears and Charles Rice, exrs. of the estate of Thomas Hicklin, dec. November, 1841. Monies Received: Sale Bill dated November 1, 1841.

Monies Expended: --- Eastman. (RD) November 1, 1841, (CLK) John Ralls.

155) First annual settlement of James Culbertson, adm. of the estate of Catharine Bast, dec. November term, 1841. Monies Received: Wm. Bast, Wm. Alford, Elizabeth Chapman, Wm. Pullen, Peter Bast, Adam Bast.

Monies Expended: On note on Adam Bast assigned to A. W. McMurty on October 26, 1836 and then assigned to the deceased. Cash paid to T. J. Ellis, G. Waters, A. Shutts, J. Alexander, J. Sosey, Moses Bast. (RD) November 1, 1841, (CLK) John Ralls.

156) First annual settlement of Alexander Buford and Abraham Buford, jr., exrs. of the estate of Abraham Buford, sr., dec. November term, 1841.

Monies Expended: Jul 8, 1841 cash paid to N. T. Pierce for taxes. Cash paid to Benj. Davis, Allen Brown. (RD) November 1, 1841, (CLK) John Ralls.

157) Final settlement of Gabriel Penn, adm. of the estate of Horatio Penn, dec. November term, 1841.

Monies Expended: I. L. Buchanan. (RD) November 2, 1841, (CLK) John Ralls.

158) Final settlement of William W. Cartwill, adm. of the estate of John Crocket, dec. November term, 1841.

Monies Received: Dr. McElroy, H. fagan.

Monies Expended: William Martin, Cartwill Crockett, N. T. Pierce, W. Martin, Jackson Crockett, Luke W. Watkins, John Hawkins, Alvin Menifee. (RD) November 2, 1841, (CLK) John Ralls.

159) William Priest, exr. of the estate of John Payne, dec. November term, 1841.

No names given. (RD) November 2, 1841. (CLK) John Ralls.

160) First annual settlement by James M. Leake, adm. of the estate of Joseph Pearielel, dec. December term, 1841.

Monies Received: Sale of personal property October 9, 1840. Cash received from William Leak (sic), Charles Rhodes, Henry Leake, Charles Asher, Benedick Carsies, S.T.T. Haynes, Benedick Gardiner, J. M. Leake, Rosaner L. Piereall (sic). (RD) December 6, 1841, (CLK) John Ralls.

161) Second annual settlement of French Glascock, adm. of Charles Glascock, dec. January term, 1842.

Monies Received: Cash from Joseph Chapman on December 26, 1840, Cash from Marcus Hall on December 27, 1840, Cash from Levi A. Hudson on January 1, 1841, Cash from B. Brizendine on January 1, 1841, Cash from John B. Parris on January 19, 1841, Cash from H. Hopkins on January 19, 1841, Cash from Hansford Brown on February 9, 1841, Cash from Samuel Smith on February 15, 1841, Cash from Allen Dodd on February 15, 1841, Cash from John B. Parris on February 15, 1841, Cash from William Small on February 28, 1841, Cash from Daniel

21

Brown on March 1, 1841, Cash from William Lmarr on March 7, 1841, Cash from John Biggs on April 5, 1841, Cash from John Ross on April 5, 1841, Cash from Saml. Stowers on June 25, 1841, Cash from William Lmarr on July 7, 1841, Cash from Spencer Glascock on August 30, 1841, Cash from Charles Mills on August 30, 1841, Cash from James R. Garnet on August 30, 1841, Cash from James Neal on June 1, 1841, Cash from William Lmarr on June 1, 1841, Cash from James Cochran on December 21, 1841.

Monies Expended: Josep. Gran, Zed. Merritt, Asa Glascock, K. M. Glascock, Hansford Brown, Joseph Green, --- Loverring, John R. Flowerree, Rob. H. McKay, R. Levering, N. Fuqua, Wm. H. Peake, M. Parker, Wilkinson W. Crawford, Lewis Garnet, N. T. Pierce. (RD) January 3, 1842. (CLK) John Ralls.

162)   First annual settlement of Joseph D. Tapley, adm. of the estate of Benjamin Gray, dec. February term, 1842.

Monies Expended: Lewis Tracy, Benj. Robinson, John Ralls, T. D. Tapley. (RD) February 7, 1842, (CLK) John Ralls.

163)   Elizabeth Weaver, adm. of the estate of Tilman Weaver, dec. February term, 1842.

Monies Received: William Dowell.

Monies Expended: I. L. Canterbury, H. D. Pariss, A. D. Northcutt, William Priest, A. and W. McMurty, R. H. McKay. (RD) February 7, 1842, (CLK) John Ralls.

164)   Final settlement by Richard Boulware, one of the administrators of the estate of Logan Boulware, dec. February term, 1842.

Monies Received: Mary Boulware for the hire of a slave.

Monies Expended: Elizabeth Wilson, Courtney Campbell by Strode & Clayton, A. H. Buckner, John Ralls, Wm. Wright & Horton. There was also $5.60 reserved to pay Geo.'s demand. No name was stated in this last entry. (RD) February 7, 1842, (CLK) John Ralls.

165)   Settlement of James Inlow, adm. of the estate of Peyton P. Wright. February term, 1842.

Monies Expended: Voucher to --- Wright as guardian. (RD) February 7, 1842, (CLK) John Ralls.

166)   Final settlement of William Sox, jr., adm. of John Douchimer, dec. February term, 1842.

Monies Expended: Stuart Rainow, John Ralls. (RD) February 7, 1842, (CLK) John Ralls.

167)   Settlement of Margaret M. Davis, extrx. of the estate of Robert Davis, dec. February term, 1842.

Monies Received: Malinda Davis, Catharine Davis, Adaline Davis.

Monies Expended: Robert M. Davis. (RD) April 4, 1842, (CLK) John Ralls.

168)   Annual settlement of Neal Cameron, adm. of the estate of Joshua Robb, dec. February term.

Monies Expended: Sale of S. P. Pavillion at St. Louis on May 10, 1840, Expenses to St. Louis to settle with S.S. Phelps, Mrs. Robb, Jannus Robb, Saml. Vandergriff. (RD) April 4, 1842, (CLK) John Ralls.

169) Annual settlement of Chapel Carstarphen, adm. of the estate of Wm. R. Brown, dec. April term, 1842. Monies Expended: W. & S. Thompson, Huntsberry & Walker, A. B. Combs. (RD) April 4, 1842, (CLK) John Ralls.

170) Second annual settlement of John Billings and Geo. Billings, adms. of the estate of Abraham Billings, dec. April term, 1842. No names given. (RD) April 2, 1842, (CLK) John Ralls.

171) Annual settlement of James McGee, exr. of the estate of James Lee, dec. February term, 1842. Monies Expended: James H. Campbell, William Lee, John J. Cryler, Silas Crigler, J. H. Leake. (RD) March 7, 1842, (CLK) John Ralls.

172) Second annual settlement of James Culbertson and William H. Vardeman, adm. of the estate of Richard Matson, dec. March term, 1842. Monies Received: From P.A. Labeaume on May 5, 1839, From Fisher & Rice on September 15, 1839, From Fisher and Rice on September 15, 1840, From Charles Rice on February 19, 1840, From Rueben and H. Low on February 3, 1840, From James L. Fisher on February 4, 1840, From Joseph Hardy on Janary 27, 1840, From A. McGinnis in November, 1829 (sic), From H. Northcutt, From Saul & Davis on December 25, 1840, From -- Saul in April, 1840, From -- Fisher for the hire of Wash. (slave) on February 4, 1840, From T. and I. Lear on May 3, 1840, From Fisher & Davis on September 14, 1841, From Thomas and J. Lear on January 22, 1841, From --- Fisher for the hire of Wash. (slave), From the rent of land in Marion and Ralls Counties in 1841. Monies Expended: On January 1, 1840 to --- Gerick for cap for Wash. (slave), On January 1, 1840 to --- Eastman for boots for Wash. (slave) on January 1, 1840, On December 30, 1839 to J. Sosey, On February 4, 1840 to J. L Fisher, On February 4, 1840 to J. B. Vardeman, On August 5, 1840 to James L. Fisher, On August 14, 1840 to I. Sosey, On August 14, 1840 to J. L. Fisher, On August 14, 1840 to J. L. Fisher, On November 1, 1840 to N. T. Pierce, On November 1, 1840 to D. Wilcock, On November 3, 1840 to George Fisher, On December 3, 1841 to A. T. Saul, On January 27, 1841 to G. C. Hays, On January 27, 1841 to Joseph Hardy, On February 1, 1841 to A. McMurty, On January 22, 1841 to T. and L. Lear, On June 1, 1841 to R. W. McCreary, On June 21, 1841 to Uriel Wright, On November 7, 1841 to N. T. Pierce, On September 9, 1841 to J. J. Montogmery, On September 9, 1841 to Willis M. Jameson. (RD) March 7, 1842, (CLK) John Ralls.

173) Annual settlement of Stephen Elliott, adm. of the estate of John Elliott, dec. May term, 1842.

Monies Expended: George L. Hardy, James Leake, Aaron Ely, Matthew Elliott, Richard Boulware. (RD) May 2, 1842, (CLK) John Ralls.

174) Second annual settlement of James G. Wylie, surviving administrator of the estate of William Wylie, dec. May term, 1842.

Monies Expended: R. H. Courtney, Wm. B. Wilson, Stephen Glascock, J. Patterson. (RD) May 2, 1842, (CLK) John Ralls.

175) Second annual settlement of Daniel B. Kendrick and Guilford D. Hansborough, exrs. of the estate of Harvey Wilson, dec. June term, 1842.

Monies Expended: --- Seroter, Alfred Wilson, Wm. Wilson, Thos. Brashear, John Houston (sic), John Hauston (sic). (RD) June 6, 1842. (CLK) John Ralls.

176) Annual settlement of Stephen Glascock, adm. of the estate of Harrison Glascock, dec. February term, 1842 (sic)

Monies Expended:To Simon Davis for 1839 school house subscription on November 4, 1838, To A. & W. McMurty on April 7, 1840, To G. C. Hays on February 8, 1842, To A. S. Barley and others as well as Simon Davis, assignee on May 7, 1839, To W. H. Leake on April 7, 1840, To Granville Clayton on September 11, 1841, To --- Eastman on March 13, 1840, To Hansford Brown on February 13, 1840, To A. C. Hawkins on November 13, 1839, To Russel King for coffin on June 6, 1840, To James Gerrish on March 17, 1840, To Luke Watkins on April 6, 1840, To Dr. Robert H. M'Kay on January 3, 1841, To Aaron Kendrick on March 9, 1839, To --- Brackenridge on May 19, 1840, To Jeptha Crosthwait on June 6, 1842.

Unbilled claims: James Carson, Joseph J. Aldridge, William S. Lofttan, William Shohony, Charles Glascock, C. Rice, B. W. Ralls. (RD) June 13, 1843, (CLK) John Ralls.

177) Final settlement of Robert Sloss, adm. of the estate of Joseph C. Epperson, dec. May term, 1842.

Monies Received: William C. Ford.

Monies Expended: D. Butler, I. Culbertson, James Garrish, Isaac Letter, Drury Eads, C. Carstarphen, David Rice, John Ralls, Joel Ledford, Joseph Wright, Wm. McMurty. (RD) July 5, 1842, (CLK) John Ralls.

178) Second annual settlement of James Epperson, adm. of Joel Taylor, dec. August term, 1842.

No names given. (RD) August 3, 1843, (CLK) John Ralls.

179) Second annual settlement of Otho Brashears and Charles Rice, adm. of the estate of Thomas Hicklin, dec. August term, 1842.

Monies Expended: --- McMurty, Dr. Leake, Lewis Tracy, J. S. Crosthwait, --- Kereheval, Hancesford Brown, John Seely, N. T. Pierce. (RD) August 31, 1842, (CLK) John Ralls.

24

180) Annual settlement of James D. Watson, exr. of the estate of John Watson, dec. August term, 1842.
Monies Expended: Wm. Watson, I. D. Palson, Wm. S. Seargeant. (RD) August 31, 1842, (CLK) John Ralls.
181) Second annual settlement of Stephen Glascock, exr. of the estate of Eli C. Galleher, dec. August term, 1842.
Monies Expended: --- McMurty, T. Rhodes, H. Meredith, Caleb N. Galleher, French Glascock, G. C. Hays, Chapman P. Green, I. L. Canterberry. (RD) August 31, 1842, (CLK) John Ralls.
182) Final settlement of Elizabeth Wilson, adm. of the estate of Presley Wilson, dec. September term, 1832.
Monies Expended: Matthew Fife, John F. Hawkins, S. C. Anderson, Elizabeth Wilson. Filed by her agent, J. J. Slosson, (RD) September 5, 1842.
183) First annual settlement of William Forman, adm. of the estate of Mary Parker, dec. September adjourned term, 1842.
Monies Received: William S. M'Eroy, S. Muldron, estate of Charles Glascock, dec., B. W. Horr, Joshua Mitchell, Charles Lamb.
Monies Expended: Floweree & Mennifee, F. Glascock, A. M. Williams, J. Mitchell, Wm. M. Priest, A. G. Galleher, William Forman, L. Tracy, J. S. Buckhannan, J. M. Johnston, T. Rhodes, George Waller, James S. Dimmitt, Solomon D. Parker. (RD) September 6, 1842, (CLK) John Ralls.
184) Second annual settle of Abraham Buford, adm. of the estate of John Buford, dec. September term, 1842.
Monies Expended: James Dunkin, Francis Conn, T. D. Reed, Jno. F. Hawkins, A. & W. McMurty. (RD) September 6, 1842, (CLK) John Ralls.
185) John Markle, jr. for F. I. Fealze, his guardian.
Monies Expended: O. Markles, --- Floweree, M. Daniel, James Barnet, S. Marsuson, S. Woods. (RD) October 3, 1842, (CLK) John Ralls.
186) Annual settlement of Benjamin Ely, adm. of Thomas Ely, dec. October term, 1842.
Slaves: Jack, Rachael.
Monies Expended: Mention of travel to New London and to Palmyra court in February, March and September of 1841. (RD) October 3, 1842. (CLK) John Ralls.
187) Annual settlement of Joel H. Epperson, adm. of the estate of Richard Epperson, dec. November term, 1842.
Monies Expended: Dr. McKay, Anthony Epperson, Alford Cox, Jas. Epperson, Washington Epperson, Dabney Jones, John Chitwood, William P. Young, Hays & Blair, Pathenia Epperson. (RD) November 7, 1842, (CLK) John Ralls.
188) First annaual settlement of Robert Bayley, adm. of the estate of Charles Bayley, dec. November term, 1842.

25

Monies Recieved: On a note from Charles W. Truitt due October 23, 1842, On a note from Arthur Scott due November 28, 1841, On a note from Peter Leonard due August 3, 1841, On a note from George Fisher due December 26, 1841, On a note from George Fisher due December 25, 1842, On a note from George Fisher due December 25, 1843, monies received from James Fuqua, constable.

Monies Expended: T. A. Haden, J. F. Epperson. (RD) November 7, 1842, (CLK) John Ralls.

189) Settlement of of William Priest, exr. of the estate of John Payne, dec. November term, 1842.

No names given. (RD) November 8, 1842, (CLK) John Ralls.

190) Settlement by James Creason, adm. The deceased's name was not given. November term, 1842.

Monies Received: Rice Carter, Matthew Brooks.

Monies Expended: Cash paid to Isham Winn on September 22, 1842 for the making of a coffin. (RD) November 7, 1842, (CLK) John Ralls.

191) Second annual settlement of Alexander Buford and Abraham Buford, exrs. of the estate of Abraham Burford, sr., dec. November, 1842.

Monies Expended: On April 26, 1842 to J. Ralls, On November 11, 1841 to J. J. Slosson, On August 23, 1842 to R. H. M'Kay, On January 15, 1842 to A. & W. McMurty, On December 6, 1841 to Wm. G. Johnston, On December 6, 1841 to J. Ralls, On August 5, 1842 to T. S. Purdom, On August 5, 1842 to Tho. S. Miller. (RD) November 7, 1842, (CLK) John Ralls.

192) Third annual settlement of Elizabeth Offutt, adm. of the estate of Thorton F. Offutt, dec. November adjourned term, 1842.

Monies Expended: Stephen Smith on November 12, 1840 for burial expenses, Flowerre & Neal, J. Dimmint, Mrs. Parker. (RD) December 5, 1842, (CLK) John Ralls.

193) Second annual settlement of James Culbertson, adm. of the estate of Catharine Bast. January term, 1843.

Monies Expended: J. Ralls, J. N. Griffin. (RD) January 2, 1843, (CLK) John Ralls.

194) Second annual settlement by James M. Leake, adm. of the estate of Joseph Pierceall, dec. January term, 1843.

Monies Expended: On June 8, 1841 to R. Pierceall, On June 8, 1841 to J. W. Leake, On November 1, 1841 to J. B. Gore, On November 4, 1841 to Jesse Boarman, On November 5, 1841 to R. J. Pierceall, On October 9, 1840 to Wm. Pulis, On December 18, 1840 to R. J. Pierceall, On December 18, 1840 to J. W. Leake, On December 21, 1840 to C. N. Lynch, On May 10, 1842 to J.I.T. McElory, On May 16, 1842 to Rasanna J. Pierceall. (RD) January 2, 1843, (CLK) John Ralls.

195) Annual settlement of James Inlow, adm. of the estate of P. P. Wright, dec. January term, 1843.

No names given. (RD) February 1, 1843, (CLK) John Ralls.
196) Annual settlement of Abraham Seely, adm. of the estate of Nelly Johnston, dec. February term, 1843.
No names given. (RD) February 6, 1843, (CLK) John Ralls.
197) First annual settlement of William Newland, adm. of the estate of John Ross, dec. February term, 1843.
No names given. (RD) February 6, 1843, (CLK) John Ralls.
198) Final settlement of Neal Cameron, adm. of Joshua Robb, dec. February term, 1843.
Monies Expended: D. M'Creary, Jno. Ralls, S. Buchanan, John J. Slosson. (RD) February 6, 1843, (CLK) John Ralls.
199) First annual settlement of James G. Wylie, adm. of the estate of Pleasant Cox, dec. February term, 1843.
Monies Expended: John Ralls, George W. Wallers, Harrison Adkins. (RD) February 7, 1843, (CLK) John Ralls.
200) Settlement of Elizabeth Weaver, adm. of the estate of Tilman Weaver, dec. February term, 1843.
Monies Expended: John Ralls, William Priest. (RD) February 7, 1843, (CLK) John Ralls.
201) Third annual settlement of French Glascock, adm. of the estate of Charles Glascock, dec. February term, 1843.
Monies Received: Jas. Cochran, William T. T. Swan, John R. Floweree, William Priest, Thos. Priest, Jno. M. Johnston.
Monies Expended: Lewis Garnett, Wm. Bull, J. C. Barrett, Jas. Fisher, B. McPherson, --- Smith, Jesse Carter, Jas. J. Green, S. Glascock, Wm. Beebe, William Lyager, Lucy J. Glascock, Wilkinson Crawford, Sewel Heperon, Thos. P. Norton, Hiram Glascock, George C. Hays, Maria Dodd,Jno. W. Johnston. (RD) February 3, 1843, (CLK) John Ralls.
202) First annual settlement by Samuel K. Caldwell, adm. of the estate of James D. Caldwell, dec. April term, 1843.
Monies Expended: On June 30, 1842 to Chapel Carstarphen, October 15, 1842 to Lewis Tracy, On August 12, 1842 to James Turley, On August 12, 1842 to G. C. Hays, On June 3, 1842 to Thos. A. Purdom, On August 12, 1842 to Lewis Tracy, On August 12, 1842 to Saml. M'Gowen, On January 15, 1842 to R. C. Caldwell, On December 2, 1841 to Alexr. M'Gaw, On December 4, 1841 to Benedict Little, On December 4, 1841 to H. Northcutt, On August --, 1842 to Hugh Emerson. (RD) April 3, 1843, (CLK) John Ralls.
203) Final settlement of Chapel Carstarphen, adm. of the estate of William R. Bown, dec. April term, 1843.
Monies Expended: A.B. Combs, A. & W. M'Murty, J. Garrish, G. C. Hays, John Ralls, Arthur Menefee. (RD) April 3, 1843, (CLK) John Ralls.
204) John Newton, adm. of the estate of Gerrard, Newton, dec. May term, 1843.
Monies Received: Land in Marion County mentioned.
Monies Expended: Thos. S. Wilson, N. T. Pierce, Stephen

Smith, James Taylor, James Neal, Gerrard Newton, dec., Dr. E. H. James. John Ralls, John J. Slosson. (RD) May 1, 1843, (CLK) John Ralls.

205)   First Annual settlement by James Inlow, exr. of Harvey M'Gown, dec. May term, 1843.

Notes On: Claborn Clark, Harper Wilson, David Clark, Wm. Darvel, Jeptha S. Crasthwait, John A. Woods, Benona Brice, Washington Epperson, Stephen Ems, James Bur, Robt. Sloss, Elmore Haze, James Crosthwait, John Fletcher, Thomas Brooks. (RD) May 1, 1843, (CLK) John Ralls.

206) First annual settlement of Jacob Zimmerman, exr. of the estate of Silas Crigler, dec. May term, 1843.

Monies Recieved: $206.17 cash on hand at the time of death of the deceased on May 1, 1842. Bank of Illinois mentioned.

Monies Expended: John Ralls, R. Wright. (RD) May 1,1843, (CLK) John Ralls.

207) Settlement by George Hardy, adm. of the estate of Wm. Pulis, dec. June term, 1843.

Monies Received: Benjamin Ely, Coleman D. Stone, David Blue, Thomas P. Norton. (RD) June 5, 1843, (CLK) John Ralls.

208) First annual settlement by John A. Wright and Corbin Berm, exrs. of the estate of Joseph Wright, dec. June term, 1843.

Monies Received: Abraham Liter, Job Mace, Wm. C. Wright, J. A. Wright, --- Daniel.

Monies Expended: P. N. Smith, J. Hildreth, T. A. Purdom, John Buford, dec., Wm. Krigbaum, James Hults, James Hawkins, J. Ralls, --- Markle, --- Taliaferro, Wm. Anderson, On June, 1842 to Thomas Cleaver, On June, 1842 to D. Jones, On June, 1842 to R. Vermillion, On June, 1842 to L. L. Smith, On June, 1842 to Wm. O. Young, On June, 1842 to Isaac Dreyfus, On June, 1842 to John J. Ely, On June, 1842 to --- Briggs, On June, 1842 to S. A. Wright, On January 2, 1843 to G. C. Hays, On January 2, 1843 to Dabney Jones, On January 25, 1843 to J. D. Tapley, On January 29, 1843 to N. Ledford, On February 6, 1843 to to J. Buford, adm., On February 9, 1843 to Anderson Briscoe, On September 2, 1842 to A. W. Perdew, On February 20, 1843 to Taylor Jones, On May 14, 1843 to James G. Wylie, On April 4, 1843 to J. J. Slosson, On April 8, 1843 to James Small, On April 8, 1843 to R. S. Wright, On June 6, 1843 to J. A. Wright, On June 6, 1843 to J. Ralls, On June 6, 1843 to --- Smith, On June 2, 1843 to --- Sisk, On June 2, 1843 Heath Jones, On June 2, 1843 to C. Berm, On June 6, 1843 to James S. Ledford, On June 10, 1843 to Wm. Briggs, On June 20, 1843 to J. C. Welbern, On June 20, 1843 to --- Anderson, On June 22, 1843 to J. D. Briggs, guardian of J. S. Ledford, On June 23, 1843 to Wm. C. Wright, On June 24, 1843 to S.B. Wright, assignee of A. & W. McMurty, On December 20, 1842 to J. A. Wright, On July 1, 1843 to J. A. Wright, On June 10, 1843 to R. Vermillion, On July 3, 1843 to J. C. Williams, On July 3, 1843 to S. B. Wright, On July 3, 1843 to J. A. Wright. (RD) July 3, 1843, (CLK) J. Ralls.

209) First annual settlement by James Epperson, adm. of the estate of Margaret Ann Mills, dec. David Mills was the former administrator. May term, 1843.

Monies Expended: James Epperson, William R. Gilbert, Thoms G. Mills, Tyre A. Haden, James Shohong, John Ralls. (RD) July 3, 1843, (CLK) John Ralls.

210) Settlement of Margaret M. Daivs, adm. of the estate of her late husband, Robt. Davis, dec. June term, 1843.

Heirs on April 4, 1842: Malinda Davis, Catharine Davis, Adaline Davis, Robert M. Davis. (RD) July 10, 1843, (CLK) John Ralls.

211) Third annual settlement of Daniel B. Kendrick and Guilford D. Hansborough, exrs. of the estate of Harvey Wilson, dec. May term, 1843.

Monies Expended: Narcissus Wilson, G. L. Hardy, Thos. Brashears, N. T. Pierce, Martin Lyle, Stephen T. Elliott, D. Kendrick, Elizabeth Wilson, John Ralls. (RD) July 10, 1843, (CLK) John Ralls.

212) Final settlement of James Epperson. adm. of the estate of Joel Taylor, dec. August term, 1843.

No names given. (RD) August 7, 1843, (CLK) John Ralls.

213) Settlement of James D. Watson, exr. of John Watson, dec. August term, 1843.

No names given. (RD) August 7, 1843, (CLK) John Ralls.

214) Annual settlement of Benjamin (last name not given-probably - Ely), adm. of the estate of Thomas Ely, dec. August term, 1843.

Monies Expended: G. L. Hardy. (RD) August 7, 1843, (CLK) John Ralls.

215) First annual settlement of John F. Leake and George L. Hardy, exrs. of the estate of James Leake, dec. August, 1843.

Monies Received: Y. L. Anderson, J. B. Leake.

Insolvent Notes on May 21, 1842: E. Poindexter, William Meteers, Robert Irwin, Benjamin Lee.

Monies Expended: On July 9, 1842 to L. S. Anderson for coffin, On October 14, 1842 to B. Rolandoe, clergyman, On July 16, 1843 to Dr. McLroy, On July 12, 1843 to John D. Biggs, On July 28, 1843 to C. N. Lynch and E. L. Bell, On July 28, 1843 to Benjamin Ely, On July 28, 1843 to J. S. Crasthwait, On August 5, 1843 to Otho Brashear, On Febryar 4, 1843 to F. Bowles, On June 10, 1843 to R. M. Brashears, On June 10, 1843 to William Leake, as an heir, On June 10, 1843 to James B. Leake, as an heir, On August 9, 1843 to James F. Mahan, June 10, 1842 to Wm. Leake, On June 10, 1842

John Blue. (RD) August 14, 1843, (CLK) John Ralls.

216)   First annual settlement of James Culbertson, adm.
of Isaac Bast, dec.   October, 1843.

Monies Received: Adam Bast, William Alfred, Willis M.
Jamison, Casper Hardy, One account on Peter and George Bast
dated 1820 and 1821, Peter Bast, Thomas Mayhall, Simeon Davis, Moses Bast, George Bast.

Monies Expended: Moses Bast, Catharine Bast, Samuel W.
Mayhall, William Bast, Lewis Tracy, John L. Smith, Willis M.
Jamison, John Ralls, Isaac Bast, French Glascock, Casper
Hardy, John Thomas Mayhall, Peter & George Bast, (RD) Octo-
ber 2, 1843, (CLK) John Ralls.

217) Final settlement of Raphael Leake, adm. of the estate of John R. Gillespie, dec. August adjourned term, 1843.

Monies Expended: Wm. C. Gillespie; On January, 1840 to
Wm. Maddox; On January, 1840 to Joseph Pierceale; On January
25, 1843 to Wm. C. Gillespie; On November, 1842 to Wm. C.
Gillespie; On August 6, 1838 to Saml. Smith; On July 5, 1842
to Dr. Jett;   On March, 1840 to Wm. Gillespie on a suit before Richd. Boyer; On March 6, 1843 to N. Shannon, J. Ralls,
B. Davis, R. Wright. (RD) October 2, 1843, (CLK) John Ralls.

218)   Second annual settlement of Joel H. Epperson, adm.
of the estate of Richard Epperson, dec. November term,
1843.

Monies Expended: On November 12, 1842 to Dr. Welbourn;
On June 19, 1843 to Jacob Sasey; On May 21, 1843 to James
Epperson; On September 12, 1843 to Peter Smelson; On August
8, 1843 to James Epperson;   On August 8, 1843 to Anthony
Epperson; On August 8, 1843 to Richard Epperson;   On August
8, 1843 to Parthenia Epperson; On August 8, 1843 to Edmund
Bailey, guardian for William Epperson; On July 1, 1843 to
John Epperson;   On August 8, 1843 to Little Berry Epperson;
On August 8, 1843 to Samuel Epperson; On November 6, 1843 to
William S. Lofland; On November 6, 1843 to John Ralls.

Bad Notes: James Eals, George Eals, Squire Brothers, A.
C. Hawkins, James M. Creason, William Fuqua, Samuel McGowen,
Luke W. Watkins. (RD) November 6, 1843, (CLK) John Ralls.

219)   Annual settlement of Henry C. Wolfe, adm. of the
estate of Ira Sheckle, dec. November term, 1843.

Monies Received: R. Redish, James Figgon. (RD) November
6. 1843, (CLK) John Ralls.

220) Second annual settlement of Robert Baley, adm. of
Charles Baley, dec. November term, 1843.

Monies Expended: Robert Bayley (sic), George Fisher,
James Shohony, jr., Edmund Baley, Isham R. Winn, Jacob
Rouland, John Ralls, (RD) November 6, 1842, (CLK) J. Ralls.

221) Settlement of William Forman, adm. of the estate of
Mary Parker, dec. November term, 1843.

Monies Expended: Henry Collins, James & Meredith, James

Withers, William   R. Harris, Jacob Long, French Glascock,
James S. Dimmitt, David Ford's admr., Hannah Tapley, Wm.
Forman, A. & W. Mc Murty, Hays & Blair, Thomas Cleaver, S.
McPherson, J. V. D. Bergen, Simon   Davis, Jos. Rice, J. R.
Garrett. (RD) November 7, 1843, (CLK) John Ralls.
    222)   Chas. F. Clayton, agent, makes a statement for the
administrator. However neither the deceased nor the admi-
nistrator's name appears in the statement. November term,
1843.
    Monies Expended: J. Sasey, French Glascock, Jno. J. Camp-
bell, Jacob Sasey. (RD) November 7, 1843, (CLK) John Ralls.
    223)   Third annual settlement of Jeremiah B. Vardeman and
William H. Vardeman, executors of the estate of Jeremiah
Vardeman, dec. November term, 1843.
    Monies Expended: Peter Smelson, Dr. James, Dr. Meredith,
William Shuck, G.C. Hays, Moses Bast, Thomas O. Rhodes. (RD)
November 7, 1843, (CLK) John Ralls.
    224)   Annual settlement of John Newton, amd. of the es-
tate of Gerrard Newton, Dec. November Adjourned term, 1843.
    Monies Expended: J. S. Buchanan, R. Wright. (RD) January
1, 1844, (CLK) John Ralls.
    225)   First annual settlement of Matthew T. Barkley and
James A. Emison, adms. of the estate of Matthew Barkley,dec.
February term, 1844.
    Monies Received: James C. Beaty, Abraham Buford's estate.
    Monies Expended: James C. Beaty, G. C. Hays, Dr. Leake,
Waller & Tracy, J. A. Emison, M. T. Barkley. (RD) February
5, 1844, (CLK) John Ralls.
    226)   Settlement of Elizabeth Weaver, adm. of the estate
of Tilman Weaver, dec. February term, 1844.
    Monies Expended: Isham O. Winn. (RD) February 5, 1844.
    227)   William Priest, exr. of the estate of John Payne,
dec. February term, 1844.
    Monies Expended: Charlotte T. Arnold. (RD) February 5,
1844, (CLK) John Ralls.
    228)   Final settlement of Abraham Seely, adm. of the
estate of Nelly Johnson, dec. February term, 1844.
    Monies Expended: On July 15, 1840 to Elijah Ling, On Au-
gust 12, 1840 to Parker Norvel, On March 7, 1842 to John
Seely, On March 29, 1842 to John Watt, On May 23, 1842 to
Richard Chitwood, On July 10, 1842 to George Seely, On February 13, 1843 to C. James, On February 13, 1843 to James
James, On April 14, 1843 to William Carson, On October 23,
1843 to Joseph T. Bowles, On March 4, 1842 to Washington
Turmer, (RD) February 5, 1844, (CLK) John Ralls.
    229)   First annual settlement of George C. Frazer and
Lucy Frazer, adms. of the estate of Thomas Frazer, dec.
March term, 1844.
    Monies Expended: J. Bell, --- Lynch, Hays & Gore. (RD)

31

March 14, 1844, (CLK) John Ralls.

230) Second annual settlement of by George C. Frazer and Lucy Frazer, adms. of the estate of Thos. Frazer, dec. March term, 1844.

Monies Expended: --- McElroy, --- Lynch, Jessy Bowman, --- Hays, --- Gore, John Ralls. (RD) March 4, 1844, (CLK) John Ralls.

231) Second annual settlement of James J. Creason, adm. of the estate of Mildred Rogers, dec. February term, 1844.

Monies Expended: On December 6, 1841 to J. D. Watson, On June 12, 1843 to John Ralls, On February 5, 1844 to Harvy Williams. (RD) February 6, 1844, (CLK) John Ralls.

232) First annual settlement of Abraham Selly, adm. of Washington Turner, dec. March term, 1844.

Monies Received: D. Jones.

Monies Expended: William Wright, Lucy Turner, Joel Ledford, Dabney Jones, W. O. Young. (RD) March 4, 1844, (CLK) John Ralls

233) Final settlement by Stephen M'Pherson, adm. of the estate of Eli C. Galleher, dec. March term, 1844.

Monies Expended: James Garrish, Robert Buchanan, Thomas Hudson, Francis Richmond, J. S. Buchanan, James Glascock, William L. Yeager, William L. Wilson, Mary Galleher, Thomas O. Rhodes, R.B. Settle, Dr. Offutt, --- Eastman, John Ralls. (RD) March 5, 1844, (CLK) John Ralls.

234) Final settlement of Stephen C. Elliott, adm. of John Elliott, dec. March term, 1844.

Monies received: Dr. Williams, Land sold to Wm. Muldrow and deed to Lillard (sic).

Monies Expended: On May 7, 1842 to Matthew Elliott, On May 20, 1842 to Matthew Elliott, On June 6, 1842 to John Ralls, On May 1, 1842 to Matthew Elliott, On June 20, 1840 to Jesse Boarman, On June 20, 1840 to Otho Brashears, On August 27, 1842 to Jesse Boarman, On July 28, 1843 to J. S. Buchanan, On July 11, 843 to Matthew Elliott, On May 2, 1842 to Lawson Berry, On May 2, 1842 to Matthew Elliott, On December 8, 1843 to Matthew Elliott, On September 28, 1842 to Matthew Elliott. (RD) March 5, 1844, (CLK) John Ralls.

235) Fourth annual settlement of French Glascock, adm. of Charles Glascock, dec. April term, 1844.

Monies Received: Robert Briggs, Charles Bohannan, John R. Floweree, James Cochran.

Monies Expended: M. McFarland, Mary Parker, -- McMurty, G. C. Hays, assignee of Robert M'Kay. (RD) April 8, 1844, (CLK) John Ralls.

236) Annual settlement by Cornelius N. Lynch, adm. of the estate of William Lynch, dec. May term, 1844.

Monies Received: On note on J. B. Gore to mature March 18, 1843, Dec. 6, 1844 $15.28 came into my hands that W. L.

Lynch loaned some man in Shelby Co. Sold a sorrel mare on December 6, 1844 to C. N. Lynch.
Monies Expended: John W. Long, Dr. Williams, James Bell, J. A. Paulding, Esq. Hardy, Esq. Elliott, N.T. Pierce. (RD) May 6, 1844, (CLK) John Ralls.

237) Second annual settlement of James Epperson, adm. of the estate of Margaret Ann Mills, dec. May term, 1844.
Monies Received: A demand against the estate of David Mills, dec.
Monies Expended: George Fisher for John Ralls, Albert Bell, John N. Mills and Thomas G. Mills, Edmund Baley, Tho. G. Mills. (RD) May 6, 1844, (CLK) John Ralls.

238) Second annual settlement of George L. Hardy, adm. of the estate of William Pulis, dec. May term, 1844.
Monies Received: On May 9, 1842 note on Benjamin Ely. Cash from David Blue, David Pulis, Thos. P. Nortin, Coleman D. Stone.
Monies Expended: May 6, 1842 delivery of personal property to Widow. Seven days service to June 5, 1843. On August 9, 1843 to J. P. Ament, Account on Benjamin Ely and David Blue. (RD) May 6, 1844, (CLK) John Ralls.

239) Settlement of James Glascock, adm. of Lucy Glascock, dec. May term, 1844.
Monies Expended: James Glascock, James W. Galleher, Voluntine P. Maston, Hiram Glascock.(RD) May 6, 1844, (CLK) John Ralls.

240) First annual settlement of Voluntine P. Matson, adm. of the estate of Lucy Glascock, dec. May term, 1844.
Monies Received: Note on William M. Daniel dated February 15, 1843, On note on James Lampkin dated January 20, 1840. (RD) May 6, 1844, (CLK) John Ralls.

241) First annual settlement of Turner Haden, adm. of the estate of Peter Leonard, dec. May term, 1844.
Monies Received: Estate of David Mills, Estate of Loyed Ford, Estate of James Baily.
Monies Expended: On April 22, 1844 to Dr. Dunkin, On July 18, 1843 to Baily & Jones, On June 14, 1843 to J. P Ament, On May 19, 1843 to R. Wright, On May 19, 1843 to John K. Hawkins, On May 19, 1843 to E. Baily, On May 19, 1843 to Curtis Carter. (RD) May 7, 1844, (CLK) John Ralls.

242) Final settlement of James Culbertson, adm. of the estate of Catharine Bast, dec. June term, 1841.
Monies Expended: J. Sasy, J. Ralls, Moses Bast, (RD) June 3, 1844, (CLK) John Ralls.

243) First annual settlement of John Bowling, dec. Adminstrator's name not stated. June term, 1844.
Monies Expended: William Tracy, Wm. Halsey, F. Meredith, John Ralls, H. H. Cohin, N. T. Pierce, John Jamison, (RD) June 3, 18444, (CLK) John Ralls.

244) Fourth annual settlement of Guylford (sic) D. Hansbrough and Daniel D. Kendrick, exrs. of the estate of Harvey Wilson, dec. June term, 1844.

Monies Expended: On September 1, 1843 to Narcissus Wilson, On April 6, 1844 to Narcissus, On April 25, 1850 to J. S. Buchanan. (RD) June 4, 1844, (CLK) John Ralls.

245) Third annual settlement of Alexander Buford and Abraham Buford, exrs of the estate of Abraham Buford, sr., dec. June term, 1844.

Monies Received: On April 5, 1840 for the sale of the land and negroes.

Monies Expended: On June 3, 1841 to Hugh Emerson; On November, 1843 to R. U. Lyons; November, 1843 to H. Brown; On May 10, 1842 to James A. Emerson; On November 21, 1843 to Peake & McKay; On November 6, 1843 to C. Carstarphen; On November 6, 1843 to G. C. Hays; On May 10, 1843 to James Dunrum; On November, 1842 to Hays & Blair; On April 8, 1844 to James Culbertson; On April 8, 1844 to G. C. Hays; On November, 1843 to N. T. Pierce; On July 11, 1843 to John Jamison; On July 11, 1843 to William L. Yager; On December, 1842 to J. Jamison; On September 6, 1842 to R. F. M'Kay; On September 6, 1842 to Hays & Blair; On October, 1843 to Thos. Crutcher; On May, 1843 to Thomas Crutcher; On November 6, 1843 to L. B. Young; On November 6, 1843 to G. C. Hays; On November 7, 1843 to Hays & Blair; On November 7, 1843 to John Ralls; In 1842, 1843, 1844 to M. Barkly & Eastman; On June 4, 1843 to Joseph Tapley; On March 10, 1842 to Sinclair Kirtley. (RD) June 4, 1844, (CLK) John Ralls.

246) Annual settlement of Branch Hatcher, adm. of S. P. Cook, dec. September term, 1843. (sic)

Monies Expended: Schooling, boarding and clothing for Elizabeth Mary Jane and Ann Eliza Cook. (RD) September 6, 1843 (sic), (CLK) John Ralls.

247) Final settlement of James Culbertson, adm. of the estate of Catharine Bast, dec. June term, 1844.

Monies Expended: J. Sasey, J. Ralls, Moses Bast. (RD) June 3, 1844, (CLK) John Ralls.

248) First annual settlement of the estate of John Bowling, dec. The administrator's name is not stated. June term, 1844.

Monies Expended: On June 30, 1844 cash was paid to William Tracy, --- Hilleredith, John Ralls, N. T. Pierce, H. H. Cohin, John Jamison (RD) June 3, 1844, (CLK) John Ralls.

249) Fourth annual settlement of Guylford D. Hansborough and Daniel B. Kendrick, adm. of the estate of Harvey Wilson, dec. June term, 1844.

Monies Expended: On September 1, 1843 to Narcissus Wilson; On April 6, 1844 to Narcissus Wilson, On April 5, 1840 to O. S. Buchanan. (RD) June 4, 1844, (CLK) John Ralls.

250) Third annual settlement of Alexander Buford and Abraham Buford, exrs. of the estate of Abraham, sr., dec. June term, 1844. On page 144 and on page 148 of Vol. One, was a statement for the third annual settlement. Both statements are included.

Monies Expended: On June 3, 144 to Hugh Emerson; On Numvember, 1843 to R. W. Lyons; On November, 1843 to H. Brown; On May 10, 1842 to James A. Emison; On November 24, 1843 to Peake & McKay;On November 6, 1843 to C. Carstarphen; On November 6, 1843 to G. C. Hays; On May 10, 1843 to Dunkin; On November, 1842 to Hays & Blair;.On April 8, 1844 to James Culbertson; April 8, 1844 to G. C. Hays; On November, 1843 to N. T. Pierce; On July 11, 1843 to John Jamison; On July 11, 1843 to William L. Yager;On December, 1842 to J. Culberson; On September 6, 1842 to R.H. McKay; On September 6, 1842 to Hays & Blair;On October, 1843 to Thomas Crutcher; On May, 1843 to Thomas Crutcher; On November 6, 1843 to D. B. Young; On November 6, 1843 to G. C. Hays; On November 7, 1843 to Hays ; On November 7, 1843 to John Ralls; In 1842 and 1843 to M. Barkly and --- Eastman; On June 4, 1844 to Joseph Tapley; On March 13, 1843 to Sinclair Kertley. (RD) June 4, 1844, (CLK) John Ralls.

251) First annual settlement of Samuel K. Caldwell and Robert B. Caldwell, adms. of the estate of Walter Caldwell, dec. May Adjourned term, 1844.

Monies Received: Saml. W. Mayhall, John P. Caldwell, Wm. Caldwell, James Mosley.

Monies Expended: On June 12, 1842 cash paid to Samuel W. Mayhall, N. T. Pierce, John Glascock. (RD) July 1, 1844, (CLK) John Ralls.

252) Final settlement of James Culbertson, adm. of the estate of Catharine Bast, dec. June, 1844.

Monies Expended: J. Sasey, J. Ralls, Moses Bast. (RD) June 3, 1844, (CLK) John Ralls.

253) Settlement of James D. Watson, exr. of John Watson, dec. August term, 1844.

Monies Expended: John Blockman. (RD) November 6, 1844, (CLK) John Ralls.

254) Second annual settlement of Taylor Jones, adm. of the estate of George Layne, dec. September term, 1844.

Monies Expended: On September 1, 1843 to --- Morris for tuition for Sarah Jane Layne; On October 20, 1843 for shoes for Polly and Patsy Layne, On April 2, 1844 to T. Force for tuition of Martha and Polly Layne. (RD) September 2, 1844, (CLK) John Ralls.

255) First annual settlement of Y. F. Hawkins, adm. of the estate of Elijah Hawkins, dec. September term, 1844.

Monies Received: Sale bill dated April 16, 1842.

Monies Received: Benj. Robinson, Jeff. S. Jamison, Uriel

Wright, -- Croswraith, Y. B. Leach, H. Elder, R. Rodes. (RD) November 16, 1844. (CLK) John Ralls, (DPY) E.W. Southworth.

256) Annual settlement of Benjamin Ely, adm. of the estate of Thomas Ely, dec. September term, 1844.

Monies Expended: On April, 1844 on execution to Cary Forman, assignee of T. L. Anderson; On May, 1844 to Jas. Leake of Saline township in favor of Cary Forman, assignee of Tho. L. Anderson; On April, 1844 to Jas. Leake, const. of Saline township, on execution in favor of W. L. Lipscomb, assignee of Samuel Glover; On March, 1844 to N.T. Pierce. (FD) September 2, 1844, (RD) November 16, 1847. (CLK) John Ralls, (DPY) E. W. Southworth.

257) Second annual settlement of James Culbertson, adm. of the estate of Isaac Bast, dec. September term, 1844.

Monies Expended: Adm. of the estate of Catharine Bast, dec.; A. McMurty; G. C. Hays; J. Alexander. (FD) October 7, 1844, (RD) November 16, 1847, (CLK) John Ralls, (DPY) E. W. Southworth.

258) Wm. Ely, adm. of the estate of Silus (sic) Crigler, dec.

Monies Received: Isaac A. Tanner, U. House.

Monies Expended: John H. Leake, John S. Spralswell, mention of settling business in Kentucky. (FD) October 7, 1844, (RD) November 16, 1847, (CLK) John Ralls, (DPY) E. W. Southworth.

259) Settlement of Thomas P. Wilson, adm. of the estate of James C. Wilson, dec.

Monies Recieved; Gabriel Penn, James L. Wood. (FD) Oct0ober 1, 1844, (CLK) John Ralls.

260) Final settlement of Margaret M. Davis, adm. of the estate of Robert Davis, dec. October term, 1844.

Monies Expended: On July 10, 1843 to the heirs of Catharine Davis, Adaline Davis, Malinda Davis; On October 5, 1844 to A. S. Aarcher (sic). (FD) October 8, 1844, (RD) November 1, 1847, (CLK) John Ralls, (DPY) WE. W. Southworth.

261) Second annual settlement of John A. Wright and Corbin Benn, exrs. of the estate of Joseph Wright, dec. July term, 1844.

Monies Expended: On July 5, 1843 to Wm. Boggs, On July 5, 1843 to C. C. Fuqua, On July 5, 1843 to C. C. Smith, On August 5, 1844 to Corbin Benn, On August 5, 1844 to J. Smith and W. C. Wright, On July 12, 1843 to C. C. Smith, On August 13, 1843 to C. C. Smith, On June 10, 1843 to H. P. Smith, On August 24, 1843 to Isaac L. Wilson, On October 26, 1843 to G. C. Hays and James Small, On October 1, 1843 -- Biggs (guardian receipt mentioned), On August 1,1843 to J.C. Nichols, On March 1, 1843 to Thomas Cleaver, On December 16, 1843 to J. C. Wellbourn, On December 3, 1843 to N. T. Pierce, On December 23, 1843 to --- Buchannan, On January 1, 1844 to John Biggs and Taylor Jones, On June 10,1843 to H. Brown, On January 12, 1844 to J. D. V. Bergen, On April 3, 1844 to Dabney Jones, On May 23, 1844 to John L. Smith, On August --, 1843 to John Ralls, On April 24, 1844 to N.T. Pierce, J. W. Mayhall and J. C. Welbourn (for Peter), On February 6, 1844 to J. D. Tapley, On February 10, 1844 to John D. Biggs, On May 29, 1844 to J. D. Wright. (FD) October 8, 1844, (RD) November 7, 1844, (CLK) John Ralls, (DPY) E. W. Southworth.

262) Final settlement of James J. Creason, adm. of the estate of Mildred Rogers, dec. November term, 1844.

Monies Expended: John C. Welborn, Js. Buchannon, Samuel G. Ewing, Willis Whitley, Jos. Fuqua, Walker Carter, John J. Slosson, John Ralls. (FD) November 5, 1844, (RD) November 17, 1847, (CLK) John Ralls, (DPY) E. W. Southworth.

263) First annual settlement of William Stears, adm. of the estate of Holliday Stears, dec. November term, 1844.

Monies Received: On January 1, 1844 from the sale of the negro girl, Harriet.

Monies Expended: J. D. Field, Rohn Ralls, J. P. Hunt. (FD) November 5, 1844, (RD) November 17, 1847, (CLK) John Ralls, (DPY) E. W. Southworth.

264) First annual settlement of William Stears, adm. of the estate of Sarah Stears, dec.

Monies Received: Sale of personal property on November 1, 1843.

Monies Expended: Edmund Bailey, Isham and Thomas Winn, Jno. W. Hemphill, Joseph Archanbeau, Bonnell & Cooper, Kethata Nowland, Jacob Nowland, Arthur Scott, Joseph Peter, J. Ralls, Milton Scott. (FD) November 5, 1844, (CLK) John Ralls, (DPY) E. W. Southworth.

265) Final settlement of William Forman, adm. of the estate of Mary Barker, dec. November term, 1844.

Monies Expended: On November 1, 1843 to James N. Garnett, On January 1, 1844 to James N. Garnett, On January 1, 1844 to Hannah Tapley, On November 1, 1844 to Hannah Tapley, On November 29, 1844 to James S. Dimmitt, On November 8, 1843 to William On November 7, 1844 to John Ralls. (FD) November 5, 1844, (CLK) John Ralls, (DPY) E. W. Southworth (Deputy Clerk's name was crossed over.)

266) First annual settlement of Benjamin Northcut, adm. of the estate of William Bainard, dec. December term, 1844.

No names given. (FD) December 2, 1844, (RD) NOvember 18, 1847, (CLK) John Ralls, (DPY) E. W. Southworth.

267) First annual settlement of Drury Eads, exr of the estate of John Dooley, dec. December term, 1844.

Monies Received: Sale of personal property on November 13, 1843.

Monies Expended: Betsy Eads; On November 13, 1843 to Js.
Crosthwait and C. Rice; On September 6, 1843 to Js. Buchannon; On November 13, 1843 to Thomas Dooley; On November 30,
1843 to J. C. Welborn; On November 30, 1843 to Thos. Dooley;
On January 22, 1844 to Thos. Dooley; On January 19, 1844 to
James Hulls; On February 5, 1844 to Wm. H. Peake; On February 5, 1844 to John D. Biggs; On April 23, 1844 to Thomas
Dooley; On November 20,1843 to Mary Dooley; On June 24,1844
to Betsy Eads; On October 9, 1844 to Betsy Eads; On July 14,
1844 to Thomas Dooley; On August 23, 1844 to Thomas Dooley;
On September 23, 1844 to Thomas Dooley; On November 29, 1844
to Thomas Dooley; William F. Tredway. (FD) December 2, 1844,
(RD) November --, 1847, (CLK) John Ralls, (DPY) E. W. Southworth.

268) Second annual settlement of Henry C. Wolfe, adm. of
the estate of Ira Scheckle, dec. December term, 1844.

Monies Expended: On November 10, 1843 to J. Green, In
1843 to Dr. McElroy; On July 21, 1844 to Thomas Campbell; On
October 25, 1843 to James Underwood; On November 4, 1844 to
H. Fagan; On November 30, 1844 to J. Bauman; On October 4,
1844 to Esq. Abbey. (FD) December 2, 1844, (RD) November
19, 1844 (sic) (?), (CLK) John Ralls, (DPY) E.W. Southworth.

269) First annual settlement of Stephen McElroy, adm. of
the estate of Charles Bohannan, dec. December term, 1844.

Monies Received: On January 12, 1844 from Wm. McFarland
for a negro boy, Silas; On January 20, 1844 from Zephanah
Kutt for a negro boy, Megres; cash from Jas. Cochran.

Monies Expended: On January 15, 1844 to --- Buchannon;
On December 23, 1843 to --- Jamison; J. M. Johnson; French
Glascock; John Floweree; Joseph Dodd; A. Cacts; Wm. Maddox;
Wm. McFarland; J. C. Brown; John Walls. (FD) December 2,
1844, (RD) November 17, 1844 (sic) (?), (CLK) John Ralls,
(DPY) E. W. Southworth.

270) Settlement of Jas. C. Bower, adm. of the estate of
Peter Bast, dec. January term, 1845.

Monies Received: Moses Richardson, G. H. & K. C. Shackleford; F. Harlinger & H. Slutter; Estate of Isaac Bast,
dec.; J. Tullake; Paulding Smith; Timothy Barney; Geo. Bast;
David Bast; Seltzer & Koller.

Monies Expended: Moses Richardson; G. H. & K. C. Shack-
leford; F. Harlinger & H. Slutter; Timothy Barney; James
McPike; David Bast; Elijah Hutson; F. M. Boyer; Mrs. Dodd;
Robert Kavanuagh; Stephen McPherson; Samuel B. Caldwell; Wm.
Reading; C. Carstarphen; Hansford Brown; William L. Yager;
R. King; James Smith; Jno. F. Wise; James Culbertson, Isaac
Bon; Stephen McPherson; William Tracy; Francis Jett; James
S. Dimmitt; John M. Johnson; Thomas Gregory; Jas. C. Bower.
(FD) January 6, 1845, (CLK) John Ralls.

271) First annual settlement of E. T. Bell, adm. of the

estate of Jas. Bell, dec. January term, 1845.
Monies Received: Jesse Bauman, Chas. Eads, H. Brown, ---
Lynch; B. Gardiner, Wm. Little, Keathly, G. L. Hardy, Brown
Tree. (CLK) John Ralls, (RD) ?.

272) First annual settlement of Wm. Stone, adm. of the
estate of Augustus P. Traske, dec. January term, 1845.
Monies Expended: A. Smith, K. J. Johnston, John Ralls,
-- Meddle, C. Wist, J. Combs, -- Roach, -- Buckhannon, A. W.
Lamb, G. Gentry and the widow. (FD) January 6, 1845, (RD)
November 22, 1847, (CLK) John Ralls, (DPY) E. W. Southworth.

273) Second annual settlement of Samuel H. Caldwell,
adm. of the estate of Robert B. Caldwell, dec. November
term, 1844.
Monies Expended: Elizabeth Watson. (FD) January 7,
1845, (RD) November 22, 1847. (CLK) John Ralls, (DPY) E. W.
Southworth.

274) Annual settlement of Mahala Glascock, adm. of the
of Thomas Glascock, dec. January term, 1845.
Monies Expended: On December 4, 1843 to R. Broughs and
W. S. Lofland; On November 10, 1843 to B. F. Darst; On November 9, 1843 to Dabney Jones; On November 18, 1843 to Wm.
O. Young; On October 17, 1843 to John Ralls; On April 10,
1844 to R. Vermillion and J. Dreyfus; On November 30, 1844
to J. Dunkum; On December 12, 1844 to J. Jamison; On January
7, 1845 to E.(?) H. McKay and H. Brown. (FD) January 7,1845,
(RD) November 22, 1847, (CLK) John Ralls, (DPY) E. W. Southworth.

275) Third and final settlement of George E. Frazier and
Leway (?) Frazier, adm. of the estate of Thos. Frazier, dec.
January term, 1845.
No name given. (FD) February 3, 1845, (RD) November 22,
1847, (CLK) John Ralls, (DPY) E. W. Southworth.

276) Second annual settlement of Abraham Seely, adm. of
the estate of Washington Turner, dec. February term, 1845.
Monies Expended: John Tapley, R. H. Mackay. (FD) February 8, 1845, (RD) November 22, 1847, (CLK) John Ralls, (DPY)
E. W. Southworth.

277) Final settlement of James M. Leake, adm. of the es-
tate of Joseph Pierceall, dec. February term, 1845.
Monies Expended: Thomas G. Gardner, Joshua Ely, Rosan J.
Pierceall, J. S. Buchannan, John Ralls. (FD) February 3,
1845, (RD) November 22, 1847, (CLK) John Ralls, (DPY) E. W.
Southworth.

278) Annual settlement of Wm. Newland, adm. of the estate of John Meass, dec. February term, 1845.
Monies Expended: Dr. Peake, N. Meass. (FD) February 8,
1835, (RD) November 22, 1847, (CLK) John Ralls, (DPY) E. W.
Southworth.

279) Second annual settlement of Mathew T. Barkley and

James A. Edmison, adms. of the estate of Matthew Barkley, dec. February term, 1845.

Monies Expended: Joseph Rice, J. Ralls, Joseph P. Buchannan, Joseph R. Rice, Joseph P. Anders. (FD) February 3, 1845, (RD) November 22, 1847, (CLK) John Ralls, (DPY) E. W. Southworth.

280) Settlement of C. N. Lynch, adm. of the estate of William S. Lynch, dec. February term, 1845.

Monies Received: J. B. Gore.

Monies Expended: J. B. Gore, Robert Bell, Thomas Norton, Joseph Ament, Henry Lawrence. (FD) Febraury 5, 1845, (RD) November 22, 1847, (CLK) John Ralls, (DPY) E. W. Southworth.

281) Settlement of Elizabeth Weaver, adm. of the estate of Tilmon Weaver, dec. March term, 1845.

Monies Expended: William Priest. (FD) March 3, 1845, (RD) November 22, 1847, (CLK) John Ralls, (DPY) E. W. Southworth.

282) First annual settlement by French Glascock and Eliza Glascock, adms. of the estate of Asa Glascock, dec. March term, 1845.

Monies Received: Wm. Brown.

Monies Expended: J. & S. Buford, Wm. O. Young, C. Jones, Storaers & Lane, Wm. H. Peake, H. Northcutt, Peake & Strode Thomas T. Rhodes, T. A. Pardom, F. Glascock. (FD) March 7, 1845, (RD) November 23, 1847, (CLK) John Ralls, (DPY) E. W. Southworth.

283) First annual settlement of Ben A. Spalding, adm. of the estate of Abraham Andrews, dec. March term, 1845.

Monies Received: Bennard Margin, J. B. Hendrick, G. L. Hardy, John Ralls, John Boman.

Monies Expended: Col. Ralls, --- Buchannan. (FD) March 18, 1845, (RD) November 28, 1847. (CLK) John Ralls, (DPY) E. W. Southworth.

284) First annual settlement of Joshua Gentry, adm. of the estate of Rodes Gentry, dec. April term, 1845.

Monies Received: On December 28, 1842 from James H. Gentry, On December 19, 1840 from John W. Turner, On September 13, 1842 from Jonathan (?), On November 22, 1841 from John Huston, John M. Sanizer and George Sanizer.

Monies Expended: Dr. McElory, L. S. Anderson, Wid. Nancy Gentry, Jacob Fudge, John Jamison, Elisha Moore, J.J. Segle, A. Blackman, Elizabeth Gentry, John Ralls, Christy Gentry, James M. Collins, Louisa Crawford, N. T. Pierce, J. J. Haus. (FD) March 14, 1845, (RD) November 28, 1847, (CLK) J. Ralls, (DPY) E. W. Southworth.

285) First annual settlement of Hiram W. Glascock, adm. of the estate of George Settle, dec. February Adjourned term, 1845.

Monies Received: Hire of negro boy, Ezekiel.

Monies Expended: P.J. Little, Thomas Settle, Isham Winn, James L. Wood, Dr. H. Meredith, Wm. G. Johnson, Wm. Settle, Dismukes, John Ralls, John Field, Jr. R. Brorough, F. Glascock, G. D. Hawkins, H. Northcutt, Wm. Priest, -- McDonald, --- Buchannan, C. Stone, T. A. Pardom, J. C. Winn, Stephen Glascock. (FD) April 14, 1845, (RD) November 28, 1847, (CLK) John Ralls, (DPY) E. W. Southworth.

286)   Fifth annual settlement of Guilford D. Hansborough and Daniel B. Kendrick, adm. of the estate of Harvey Wilson, dec. April term, 1845.

Monies Expended: On December 2, 1844 to John Jamison; On April 26, 1844 to Geo. L. Hardy; On December 9, 1844 to Narssissus (sic) Wilson; On November 30, 1844 to James Mason; On November 6, 1844 to J. Ralls; On November 8, 1844 to Narssus (sic) Wilson; On February 7, 1845 to W. W. Williams. (FD) April 28, 1845, (RD) November 28, 1847, (CLK) J. Ralls, (DPY) S. E. Southworth.

287)   Final settlement of John Billings and George Billings, adm. of the estate of Abraham Billings, dec. May term, 1845.

Monies Expended: H. Williams, K. Francis, John Houderback, --- Hascall, H.L. Anderson, Thomas Nunn, Js. Buchanan, R. H. McKay, Buchannan & Peake. (FD) May 5, 1845, (CLK) John Ralls.

288)   Second annual settlement of Turner Haden, adm. of the estate of Peter Leonard, dec. May term, 1845.

Monies Received: Thomas G. Mills, R. Tompkins.

Monies Expended: On May 20, 1844 to Charles Scandland; On May 20, 1844 to Charles Scandland; On September 5, 1844 to W. Mace; On March 15, 1845 to James Epperson; On May 29, to William Haden; On June 6, 1844 to John Dawson; On October 25, 1844 to William Corbin; On April 14, 1845 to John C. Wellbourn; On February 12, 1845 to William Stears; On July 29, 1844 to G. C. Hays; On November 9, 1844 to John Watters; On August 20, 1844 to E. Bailey; On May 20, 1844 to Joel Epperson; On May 20, 1844 to George Campbell; On May 19, 1844 to Y. A. Haden; On July 19, 1844 to John Ralls. (FD) May 5, 1845, (CLK) John Ralls.

289)   Second annual settlement of James C. Wylie, adm. of the estate of Plesant Cox, dec. March term, 1845.

Monies Expended: Lewis Tracy, Hays & Blair, N.T. Pierce, On October 23, 1841 to Thomas Cleaver, On August 18, 1843 to W. J. Johnson, Peake & McKay, On May 2, 1842 to S. Cleaver, On November 1,1841 to S. Cleaver,On May 2, 1842 to J. Taler, On November 1, 1841 to Wm. Jones and --- Davis, On February 9, 1842 to J. L. Fisher, On October 9, 1843 to J. Ralls, On May 3, 1842 to A. C. Hawkins and to --- Shackleford. (FD) May 5, 1845, (RD) November 25, 1847, (CLK) John Ralls, (DPY) E. W. Southworth.

290)   Annual settlement of James Inlow, adm. of the estate of Peyton P. Wright, dec. May term, 1835.
Monies Expended: John A. Wright, guardian of minor heirs; Geo. Moole; --- Williams; L. Watkins. (FD) May 6, 1845, (RD) November 23, 1847, (CLK) John Ralls, (DPY) E. W. Southworth.

291)   Second annaul settlement of James Inow, adm. of the estate of Harvey McGown, dec. May term, 1845.
Monies Received: John Fletcher, Thompson Brooks, David Clark.
Monies Expended: On September 5, 1842 to Hendricks & Philips; On April 5, 1842 to F. B. Leake; On November 7, 1842 to J. S. Crosthwait; On July 28, 1843 to Joseph Evans; On July 17, 1843 to Henry Palmer; On May 3, 1844 to J. S. Crosthwaith; On April 4, 142 to Powhattan Bryan; On July 2, 1845 to John Ralls; On February 6, 1843 to Clabourn Clark.
Insolvent Notes: John Fletcher, Thompson Brooks. (FD) May 6, 1845, (RD) November 24, 1847, (CLK) John Ralls, (DPY) E. W. Southworth.

292)   First annual settlement of Mary Blue and George L. Hardy, adm. of the estate of David Blue, dec. June term, 1845.
Monies Expended: On May 2, 1844 to J. P. Ament; On April 18, 1844 to D. B. Hendricks; On April 16, 1844 to C. Brashears; On May 17, 1844 to J. Ralls; On May 17, 1844 to B. Ely; On March 12, 1844 to G. L. Hardy; On May 21, 1844 to G. L. Hardy; On December 24, 1844 to McElroy & Tapley; On October 7, 1844 to A. W. Lamb; On May 5, 1844 to J. Blue, G.L. Hardy and G. Hardy.
Insolvent Notes: John Blue, Raymond Elliott, Justin Weaver, James Clayton, Jacob Fudge. (FD) June 3, 1845, (CLK) John Ralls.

293)   First annual settlement of Hanceford Brown, adm. of the estate of Robert H. McKay, dec. July term, 1845.
Monies Received: Sale bill dated June 5, 1844.
Monies Expended: Robert H. McKay;On May 8, 1844 to J. S. Buchannan; On June 1, 1844 to Harriet Kelsey; On May 8, 1844 to Charles Kennedy; On February 10, 1845 to Wm. Tracy; On September 6, 1844 to Henry Robinson; On October 5, 1844 to George M. Waller; On May 6, 1844 to Stephen Smith; On January 6, 1845 to Benj. Brice; On December 20, 1844 to A. J. Brown; On April 9, 1845 to A. & W. McMurty; On April 9, 1845 order against Jas. C. Brown before L. J. Caldwell; On September 1, 1844 to John W. Minor; On May 1, 1845 to Jacob Harlinger. (FD) July 8, 1845, (CLK) John Ralls.

294)   Settlement of William Priest, exr. of the estate of John Payne, dec.
Monies Expended: Milton Mullins, Charles P. Combe, (FD) August 4, 1845, (CLK) John Ralls.

42

295) First annual settlement of Benjamin Ely, adm. of the estate of Aaron F. Ely, dec. August term, 1845.
Monies Received: J. Snider, Rodes Gentry, Sampson Smith, J. McElroy, James Ferrel, R. Gentry, J.F. Strode, Thos. Tip, Benj. Kendrick, Rob. Snyder, James N. Fudge.
Monies Expended: Dr. McElroy. (FD) August 2, 1845, (CLK) John Ralls.
296) Settlement of James D. Watson, exr. of the estate of John Watson, dec. August term, 1845.
Monies Expedned: John Brockman. (FD) August 4, 1845, (CLK) John Ralls.
297) Third settlement of Otho Brashear and Charles Rice, exrs. of the estate of Thomas Hicklind, dec. August term, 1845.
Monies Expended: James Hull, Samuel K. Caldwell, R. W. Hicklind (heir of the estate), Ruebin W. Hicklind, John Jamison, Israel Saecer (?), Charles Rice, --- Eastman, B. Hicklind, Thomas G. Gardiner, Otho Brashear. (FD) August 5,1845, (RD) November 25, 1847, (CLK) John Ralls, (DPY) E. W. Southworth.
298) Annual settlement of Benjamin Ely, adm. of the estate of Thomas Ely, dec. August term, 1845.
No names given and not signed by the clerk. (FD) August 5, 1845.
299) Final settlement of George L. Hardy, adm. of William Pulis, dec. November term, 1843.
Monies Expended: David Pulis, A. W. Lamb, John Ralls, Samuel Glover. (FD) November 3, 1845, (RD) November 25, 1847, (CLK) John Ralls, (DPY) E. W. Southworth.
300) Final settlement of Henry C. Wolfe, adm. of the estate of Ira Sheckels, dec. November term, 1845.
Monies Expended: John Ralls.
Insolvent Notes: J. E. Walker dated October 8, 1836. (FD) November 3, 1845, (RD) November 25, 1847, (CLK) John Ralls, (DPY) E. W. Southworth.
301) Final settlement of Taylor Jones, adm. of the estate of George Layne, dec. November term, 1845.
Monies Expended: On May 29, 1845 to Robert Layne; On June 12, 1845 to Robert Layne; On September 24, 1845 to Srah Jane Quicke or Wicke (?), On October 15, 1845 for the schooling of Patsy and Polly Ann; On October 20, 1845 to J. P. Ament; On November 3, 1845 to John Ralls. (FD) November 3, 1845, (CLK) John Ralls.
302) Second annual settlement of B. A. Spalding, adm. of Abram Anders, dec. November term, 1845.
Monies Expended: Robert Hagar, A. W. Lamb, A. Winn. (FD) November 3, 1845. (CLK) John Ralls.
303) Second annual settlement of Benjamin F. Northcut adm. of the estate of Wm. Barnard, dec. November term, 1845.

Monies Expended: John Barnard, Horace McElroy, Matthew Brooks, James Creason, O. F. Rogers, Dell Cottingham, John Gannon. (FD) November 3, 1845, (CLK) John Ralls.

304) Settlement of James Glascock, adm. of Lucy J. Glascock, dec. November term, 1845.

Monies Expended: Simon Davis,Nancy Cottle, J. Baker, (FD) November 3, 1845, (RD) November 26, 1847, (CLK) John Ralls, (DPY) E. W. Southworth.

305) Second annual settlement of James Glascock, adm. of Lucy Glascock, dec. September term, 1845. (These two entries were next to each other.)

Monies Expended: William Shelly. (FD) October 8, 1845, (RD) November 28, 1847, (CLK) John Ralls, (CLK) E. W. Southworth.

306) Third annual settlement of James T. Matson and Polly Matson, adms. of the estate of Valentine P. Matson, dec. November term, 1845.

Monies Received: Horatio Penn, G. N. Green, James Glascock, Coleman Stover, Henry Robertson, Thomas Banks, William Read, Wm. Emison, J. Glascock.

Monies Expended: H. Penn, Thomas Winn, Isaac Scearce, J. S. Buchannan, Thomas H. Bowls, William Tracy, John Jamison, F. G. Glascock, George Eals, James Glascock, Thomas M. Winn, Henry Low, James Smith and son, J. D. Watson and T. M. Winn, F. B. Stout, F. P. Glascock, Hosia Northcutt, Tho. W. Bowls, John H. Hawkins, Dolly Matson. (FD) November 3, 1845, (RD) November 27, 1847, (CLK) John Ralls, (DPY) E. W. Southworth.

307) Second annual settlement of the estate of Peter Bast, dec. November term, 1845.

Monies Received: Samuel Hays, C. Seltzer.

Monies Expended: J. B. Bower, Stephen Cleaver, (FD) November 3, 1845, (FD) November 27, 1847, (CLK) John Ralls, (DPY) E. W. Southworth.

308) Secaon annual settlement of William Stears, adm. of the estate of Sarah Stears, dec. December term, 1845.

Monies Expended: Jas. Shohonney, Wm. H. Peake, Jas. H. Fruit, Turner Haden, J. C. Wilborn, John Ralls, John Gray, H. Wellman. (FD) December 2, 1845, (RD) November 27, 1847, (CLK) John Ralls, (DPY) E. W. Southworth.

309) Second annual settlement of William Stears, adm. of the estate of Holeday Stears, dec. December term, 1845.

Monies Expended: Alexander and Sarah Drummin, John H. Stears, Samuel E. Allen and wife, Warfield Snell and wife. (FD) December 2, 1845, (RD) November 27, 1847, (CLK) John Ralls, (DPY) E. W. Southworth.

310) Final settlement of James Culbertson, adm. of the estate of Isaac Bast, dec. May term, 1845.

Monies Received: C. Bast.

Monies Expended: R. Hagar, G. Kennedy, Wm. H. Hays, J.

Sosey, George Bast. (FD) January 5, 1846, (RD) November 29, 1847, (CLK) John Ralls, (DPY) E. W. Southworth.

311) Second annual settlement of E. T. Bell, adm. of the estate of Jas. Bell, dec. January term, 1846.

Monies Expended: Susan Bell, Rob. Bell, Rich. Bell, F. Frazier, John Ralls, J. Spalding, E. Poindexter, T. P. Norton, John Small, E. T. Bell, Jst. Harvey, J. A. Emison, N. O'Biren. (FD) January 5, 1846, (RD) November 29, 1847, (CLK) John Ralls, (DPY) E. W. Southworth.

312) First annual settlement of the estate of Russel King, dec. Administrator's name is not given. January term, 1846.

Monies Expended: On November 16, 1844 to L. W. Mayhall, On December 4 1844 to G. C. Hays, On January 1, 1845 to Thomas Cleaver, On January 1, 1845 to James I. Alford, On April 14, 1845 to Jeremiah Labor, On March 3, 1845 to George Glascock, On March 15, 1845 to R. Payne, On March 25, 1845 to Robert Lyons, On May 9, 1845 to H. A. Brown, On November 25, 1845 to G. C. Hays, On December 8, 1845 to Hancsford Brown. (FD) February 2, 1846, (CLK) John Ralls.

313) Annual settlement of Landie Fagan, adm. of the estate of Gerard Fagan, dec. February term, 1846.

Monies Received: Thornton Yancy, Joshua Elzy, Benj. Ely, Hiram L. Biggs. (FD) February 2, 1846, (CLK) John Ralls.

314) Settlement of Elizabeth Weaver, adm. of the estate of Tilman Weaver, dec. February term, 1846.

Monies Expended: William Priest. (FD) February 2, 1846, (CLK) John Ralls.

315) Second annual settlement of Joshua Gentry, adm. of the the estate of Rodes Gentry, dec. February term, 1846.

Monies Expended: Ben Ely, P. P. Gentry, James Man, John D. Dawson, F. Bowls, John J. Segle, Benj. Ely, J. J. Lyle, John T. Thompson, Joel Finks, Js. Buckman, Nancy Gentry, R. A. Moffett, T. Wilson, J. Gentry, Gunn & Caldwell, C. F. Clayton, J. M. and George Smizer, James Gentry. (FD) February 2, 1846, (CLK) John Ralls.

316) Second annual settlement of Stephen McPherson, adm. of the estate of Charles Bohannan, dec.

Monies Received: Hire of negro woman, Edy to Jesse Carter for 1844.

Monies Expended: Walter McFarland, Anderson & Dryden, C. Carstarphen, Edward Hughs. (FD) February 2, 1846, (CLK) John Ralls.

317) Second annual settlement of William Stone, adm. of the estate of Augustus P. Trank. February term, 1846.

Monies Expended: A. Smith. (FD) February 2, 1846, (CLK) John Ralls.

318) Annual settlement of Branch Hatcher, adm. of the estate of S. P. Cook. February term, 1846.

45

Monies Expended: Mention of the schooling of Elizabeth. (FD) February 3, 1846. (CLK) John Ralls.

319) First annual settlement of Stephen McPherson, adm. of the estate of Zephaniah Keith, dec.

Monies Received: Sale bill dated September 28, 1844. Monies Expended: S. I. Harrison, Wm. McFarland, N. P. Hornback, J. M. Hornback, Mark Bird, Gabriel Turner, Stephen McPherson, Richd. Boyer, F. Blasar, J. S. Buchannan, John Saunders, Isaac Scearce, Luke W. Watkins, Joseph Tapley, R. Tegren. (FD) February 2, 1846, (CLK) John Ralls.

320) Final settlement of James A. Emison and Mathew T. Bradley, adm. of the estate of Matthew Barkley, dec. February term, 1846.

Monies Expended: J. P. Ament, Joseph Rice, John Ralls. (FD) February 3, 1846, (CLK) John Ralls.

321) Final settlement of Abraham Seely, adm. of the estate of Washington Turner, dec. February term, 1846.

Monies Expended: J. P. Ament, J. Ralls, B. Robins. (FD) February 8, 1846, (CLK) John Ralls.

322) First annual settlement of James Culbertson, adm. of the estate of Alexander W. Spotswood, dec. February term, 1846.

Monies Received: $58.50 cash on hand on January 22, 1845. Insolvent notes: Wm. E. Higgins, Wm. L. Tipton. Monies Expended: J. Sosey, Wm. Tracy, L.W. Watkins, John Ralls. (FD) February 3, 1846, (CLK) John Ralls.

323) Final settlement of William Maddox, adm. of the estate of David Ford, dec. March term, 1846.

Monies Expended: Ford's wife, Matilda. (FD) March 2, 1846, (CLK) John Ralls.

324) First annual settlement of Raphel Leake, adm. of the estate of Charles Rodes, dec. April term, 1845. (sic)

Monies Expended: On March 9, 1844 for burial expenses; On April 3, 1844 for clothing for none children; On May 15, 1844 for expenses of taking four children to school in St. Louis; On April 3, 1844 paid sad crier; On April 3, 1844 paid Lynch's note, and Miss Grimes' demand; On October 5, 1844 paid O'Brien's note; March paid Dr. Williams, R. Pierceall. (FD) April 14, 1845 (sic), (CLK) John Ralls.

325) Second annual settlement of Raphael Leake, adm. of the estate of Charles Rhodes, dec. April term, 1846.

Monies Expended: James T. Ha (sic), G. E. Frazer, J. A. Spalding, Matthew Elliott, James M. Leake, Dr. McElory & Tapley, William Greathouse, E. T. Bell, Clement Pierceall, J. S. Crosthwait, Casper Hardy, James M. Smith, Joshua Wilson, James Elliott, G. G. E. Frazier (sic), Mention of keeping a child for one year. (RD) April 6, 1846, (CLK) John Ralls.

326) Final settlement of James Culbertson and William H.

Vardeman, adms. of the estate of Richard Matson, dec. April term, 1846.

Monies Received: Rent of land in Marion and Ralls Counties, rent of mill to -- Hawkins, hire of the slave, Washington, sale of slave, Washington, rent of mill to -- Smith.

Monies Expended: On December 29, 1842 to L. Soasey; On March 15, 1843 to G.D. Hamilton; In 1838 to C. Carstarpehen; On October 10, 1843 to I. D. S. Dryden; On February 1, 1843 to Charles Glascock' estate; On January 11, 1843 to T. Sear; On September 15, 1843 to H. Wilson; On November 7, 1842 to A. Rellan; On November 15, 1842 to S. B. Vardeman; On June 23, 1842 to Z. Merritt; On December 20, 1842 to C. C. Fuqua; On February 7, 1842 to W. M. Jamison; On January 19, 1842 to J. Ralls; On Dece,ber 15, 1842 to S. Glascock;On February 1, 1842 to J. Ashinet; On January 1, 1843 to J. B. Vardeman; On August 16, 1842 to Fuller; On October 13, 1843 to J.K. Hawkins; On November 13, 1843 to C. Wells; On October 29, 1844 to U. Wright; On February 22, 1844 to N. T. Pierce; On January 15, 1844 to H. Brown; On September 15, 1844 to Waller & Smith; On August 12, 1844 to the guardian of James Matson; On September 1, 1845 for the release of James Matson for the sale of the slave, Washington; On May --, 1842 to W. F. Kercheval; On May --, 1842 to Wm. H. Vardeman; On August 12, 1842 to the guardian of Richd. Matson; On July 22, 1842 to Saml. Fuller. In 1839 clothing for slave, Washington; On September 15, 1845 to N. Fike.

Insolvent Notes: P. A Labeaume, loss of the mill to Smith 5 months and 17 days ago when in the possession was taken by Songram's heirs. (RD) April 6, 1846, (CLK) John Ralls.

327) Third and final settlement of William Newland, adm. of the estate of John Ross. May term 1846.

Monies Expended: Judgement for -- Well; Stephen Smith; G. C. Hays; --- Buchannan; --- Jamison; A. W. Sam. (RD) May 4, 1846, (CLK) John Ralls.

328) Third annual settlement of James Inlow, adm. of the estate of Harvey McGowen, dec. May term, 1846.

Monies Expended: Benjamin Robinson for a note between November 2, 1842 to May 4, 1846; Isaac Titer; Henry Palmer. (RD) May 4, 1846, (CLK) John Ralls.

329) First annual settlement of John D. Biggs, adm. of the estate of Robert Jamison, dec. May term, 1846.

Monies Received: For the hire and the sale of the slave, Jim.

Monies Expended: Wm. T. Bond, J. Culbertson, W.O. Young, J. Krigbaum, J. Ralls, G. C. Hays, William Tracy. (RD) May 4, 1846, (CLK) John Ralls.

330) Annual settlement of Lovel Rouse, adm. of the estate of George Rouse, dec. May term, 1846.

Monies Expended: Wm. Cranford, S. Bare, John Ralls, Adam

Utterback, Uriel Rouse, Simen Rouse, Isaac A. Tanner, Allen Rouse, Elisha Rouse, Julius Rouse, Rolen Rouse, John Millon, John Jamison, John M. Crawford, Jacob Fudge. (RD) May 4, 1846, (CLK) John Ralls.

331) Final settlement of Turner Haden, adm. of the estate of Peter Leonard, dec. May term, 1846.

Monies Received: J. Bell, W.S. Lofland, Isaac P. Willson.

Monies Expended: On January 12, 1844 to Oliver Payne; On December 15, 1845 to J. R. Fisher; On January 1, 1845 to Susan Fisher; On January 1, 1845 to S. W. Mayhall; On May 6, 1845 to John On January 7 and 19, 1846 to John Bell; On April 6, 1846 to G. Campbell; On February 11, 1846 to I Sosey and P. Dudley; On April --, 1846 to T. A. Haden; On April 7, 1846 to J. C. Wellborn; On February 13, 1846 to J. D. Field; On February 19, 1846 to Jacob Sosey; On May 5, 1846 to Isaac Scraew (?), adm., Thomas Cleaver, Hanceford Brown, Adam Mase, John Ralls and Turner Haden. (RD) May 5, 1846, (CLK) John Ralls.

332) Settlement of James D. Watson, exr. of the estate of John Watson, dec. June term, 1846.

Insolvent Notes: Bond on Hezekiah Faris due November 8, 1828; Bond on Overton D. Watson due February 13, 1838; Verbal Acceptance by William Sergeant. (RD) June 1, 1846, (CLK) John Ralls.

333) Second annual settlement of G. S. Hardy and Mary Blue, adms. of the estate of David Blue, dec. June term, 1846.

Monies Expended: May Blue, George S. Hardy, Estate of William Rules, dec., In October, 1844, grave stone purchased from Michael F. Blue. (RD) June 1, 1846, (CLK) John Ralls.

334) Final settlement of Wm. S. Ely, adm. of the estate of Silas Crigler, dec.

Monies Received: William House of Kentucky, Zimmerman's estate.

Monies Expended: A. F. Wayland, C. Crigler, Wm. S. Ely as guardian of Sylves C. H. Crigler, heir of Silas Crigler, J. Truitt, P. Ament, --- Scarce. (RD) June 1, 1846, (CLK) John Ralls.

335) Settlement of Hiram W. Glascock, adm. of the estate of George Settles, dec.

Monies Received: Elizabeth Settles for the hire of a negro woman for 1845, Samuel Elzaes for the hire of a negro boy in 1845, Peter C. Settles for the rent of the farm.

Monies Expended: Henry Priest, H. Brown as adm. of R. H. McKay, H. Wellman, Tyra A. Haden, Elizabeth Settle, G. Clayton, Jas. Fuqua. (RD) June 1, 1846, (CLK) John Ralls.

336) First annual settlement of Chapel Carstarphen, exadm. of the estate of John S. Felix, dec. July term, 1846.

Monies Expended: --- Jamison, Mrs. Felix. (RD) June 1, 1846, (CLK) John Ralls.

337) First annual settlement of Francis Coun, adm. of the estate of Mildred A. Coun, dec. August term, 1846.

Monies Expended: --- Jamison, William Tracy, J. S. Buchanan, R. W. Hicklin, N. Fuqua, -- Hurley. (RD) August 5, 1846, (CLK) John Ralls.

338) First annual settlement of James Buford, adm. of the estate of Leonard Porter, dec. August term, 1846.

Monies Expended: Taylor Jones, Peake & Strode, Jacob Saffell, C. F. Clayton, G. C. Hays. (RD) August 5, 1846, (CLK) John Ralls.

339) Second annual settlement of Benjamin Ely, adm. of the estate of Aaron F. Ely, dec. August term, 1846.

Monies Expended: McElroy & Tapley, --- Lyles, George Utterback, Isaac Ely, William Wilson, Jacob Fudge. (RD) August 5, 1846, (CLK) John Ralls.

340) Final settlement of James Epperson, adm. of the estate of Margaret Mills, dec. August term, 1846.

Monies Expended: Joseph P. Ament, Jacob Roland, Enoch Matson, John Sinclear, John D. Field, Ann Mills, George D. Tuggle, A. D. Northcutt, Squire Brothers, John Ralls. (RD) August 5, 1846, (CLK) John Ralls.

341) First annual settlement of Charles Rice, surviving adm. of the estate of Thomas Hicklin, dec. August term, 1846.

Monies Expended: R. Bronaugh, Eliza Hicklin, John Geery, Hugh Emison, George Rice, John Tapley, R. W. Hicklin, J. S. Crosthwait, Wm. Boyd, J. Jamison. (RD) August 6, 1846, (CLK) John Ralls.

342) First annual settlement of William Newland, adm. of the estate of Mary McClelalland, dec. September term, 1846.

Monies Expended: On July 28, 1845 to William Gerard, On May 25, 1845 to S. I. Harrison, On June 9, 1845 to William C. Buck, In June, 1845 to H. Gentry, and N. Newland. (RD) September 7, 1846, (CLK) John Ralls.

343) First annual settlement of John C. Dawson, adm. of the estate of James Ferrill, dec. October term, 1846.

Monies Expended: Mrs. Ferrill, J. S. Buchanan, John J. Slosson. (RD) October 5, 1846, (CLK) John Ralls.

344) First annaul settlement of Martin B. Jefferies, adm. of the estate of Joseph Jefferies, dec. October term, 1846.

Monies Received: Sale of land to Alexander Wilson. (RD) October 6, 1846, (CLK) John Ralls.

345) Final settlement of James Inlow, exr. of the estate of Harvey McGowen, dec. November term, 1846.

Monies Expended: On May 5, 1846 to H. Palmer, In May,1843 to J.M. Crosthwait. (RD) November 3, 1846, (CLK) J. Ralls.

346) Third annual settlement of Joshua Gentry, of the estate of Rodes Gentry, dec. November term, 1846.

Monies Expended: --- Caldwell, John Ralls, Chowing & Williams, Jonathan Hill, Nancy Gentry, Glover & Campbell, John Huston, Buller & Philips, Wm, Carson, J. H. Puney, R. C. & H. Martin, Morgan Barnett, Joseph Rogers, Isaac Scarce, H. Thomas. (RD) November 3, 1846, (CLK) John Ralls.

347) Final settlement of B. F. Northcutt, adm. of the estate of Wm. Barnard, dec. November term, 1846.

Monies Expended: J. Ralls, A. McMurty, Wm. Miller, John Garrison. (RD) November 3, 1846, (CLK) John Ralls.

348) First and final settlement of Chapel Carstarphen, adm. of the estate of Thomas A. Purdom, dec. November term, 1846.

Monies Expended: J. S. Buchanan, S. W. Mayhall, Samuel Smith, G. C. Hays, R. T. Holedy, Mary Buford, C. Kennedy, Martin Jefferies, Wm. E. Harris, Wilson A. Purdom, John Hawkins, D. P. Fike, E. N. Hascall, James Buford, Leonard Porter, John Ralls. (RD) November 9, 1846, (CLK) John Ralls.

349) First and final settlement of Chaphel Carstarphen, ex-adm. of the estate of John M. Kelsey, dec. November term, 1846.

Monies Expended: John Ralls. (RD) November 9, 1846, C(LK) John Ralls.

350) Final settlement of William Stears, adm. of the estate of Sarah Stears, dec. December term, 1846.

Monies Expended: Geo. C. Hays, H. Wellman. (RD) December 7, 1846, (CLK) John Ralls.

351) First annual settlement of Baylis G. Rector, adm. of the estate of Volentine P. Matson, dec. November term, 1846.

Monies Expended: On November 17, 1845 to F. B. Stout, On November 14, 1845 to J. S. Buchanan, On January 8, 1846 to D. Watson. (RD) Decmber 8, 1846, (CLK) John Ralls.

352) Final settlement of Joseph C. Bower, adm. of the estate of Peter Bast, dec. December term, 1846.

Monies Received: Est. of Isaac Bast, dec., John Jamison.

Monies Expended: J. S. Buchanan, J. Ralls. (RD) December 28, 1846, (CLK) John Ralls.

353) Second annual settlement of Mary King and James L. Alford, adms. of the estate of Russel King, dec. November term, 1846.

Monies Expended: On September 26, 1845 to G. C. Hays, On June 5, 1845 to -- Hays, On March 25, 1845 to -- Hays, On May 4, 1845 to William Steers, On December 2, 1844 to T. A. Haden. (RD) November 2, 1846, (CLK) John Ralls.

354) Final settlement of William Stone, adm. of the estate of Augustus P. Traks, dec. January term, 1847.

Monies Received: Tyre Rodes, G. Schooter.

Monies Expended: --- Dixon, --- Buchanan, A. S. Lamb,
Wm. Stone, -- Ralls. (RD) January 4, 1847, (CLK) John Ralls.
355) First annual settlement of John Siler, exr. of the
estate of John Siler, dec. December term, 1846.
Monies Received: Abraham Siler, Two notes on Christian
Siler dated February 11, 1836, One note on Isaac Siler due
November 19, 1840.
Monies Expended: William Tracy, J. S. Crosthwait, J. M.
Crosthwait, McElroy & Tapley, Jn. Ralls, J. S. Buchanan, ---
Jamison, Abraham Siler. (RD) January 4, 1847, (CLK) John
Ralls.
356) Settlement of Henry P. Smith, adm. of the estate of
Wm. Smith, dec. November term, 1846.
Monies Received: On Note on Abraham Smith of Kentucky,
Richard B. Jennings.
Monies Expended: R. B. Jennings, John Ralls, E.W. South-
worth. (RD) January 5, 1847, (CLK) John Ralls.
357) Second annual settlement of of Stephen M'Pherson,
adm. of Zephaniah Keith, dec. February term, 1847.
Monies Expended: W. W. Allen, Stephen Smith, Dr. Humph-
hreys, (RD) February 1, 1847, (CLK) John Ralls.
358) Final settlement of Elxis (sic) T. Bell, adm. of the
estate of James Bell, dec. February term, 1847.
Monies Expended: E. T. Bell, Susan Bell, John Coleman,
Wm. Forrens, David Rulis, --- Sacaset, John Ralls, Matthew
Elliott, A. Samls. (RD) February 2, 1847, (CLK) John Ralls.
359) Settlement of Hiram W. Glascock, adm. of the estate
of George Settle, dec. February term, 1847.
Monies Expended: J. S. Buchanan, J. C. Northcut, James
Glascock, James Fuqua, John H. Glascock, H. W. Glascock, J.
F. Painter, J. Smith & son, S. W. Mayhall, P. H. Wellman, J.
Ralls. (RD) February 2, 1847, (CLK) John Ralls.
360) Settlement of Mary Ann Winn, adm. of the estate of
Thomas M. Winn, dec. February term, 1847.
Monies Expended: Jacob Coffman's bill for coffin for
daughter, Dr. Hawkins, Wm. Tracy's bill for coffin of the
deceased, Dr. Comstock, Dr. C. F. Clayton, A. Curt, James
Fuqua, Hays & Hampton, Payment of the coffin of Mrs. Parson,
Estate of Volentine Matson, dec., John D. Field, George M.
Kasson, Mary Elgen, --- Meredith, Charles Scanland, Richard
Epperson, Joel Epperson. (RD) February 2, 1847, (CLK) John
Ralls.
361) Second annual settlement of Hanceford Brown, adm.
of the estate of Robert H. McKay, dec. January (sic) term,
1847.
Monies Expended: A. W. Spotswood, Jeremiah Strode, James
Mosely, Wm. Eoff, Thomas Elder, John Fanning, William Fuqua,
John Penn, Jeremiah Salor, Wm. Bass, Philip Field, Robert A.
Davis, W. M. Jamison, Mr. Miller, Mr. Bailey, George Waters,

51

Henry Low, D. C. Tuttle, Mrs. Field, Wm. Eoff, A. F. Saul, W. F. G. Sansdale, Samuel H. Hill, John W. Fuqua, Charles Markle, Reason Vermillon, James Creason, S. B. Wright, H. W. Peden, L. Bonzendine, T. S. Dodd, Wm. S. Lofland, -- Cross, Ben Northcut, Spotswood, G. Smith, Samuel Inlow, W. A. Maddox, G. M. Waller, Mrs. H. Bahannan, G. M. Waller, Isham O. Winn, Russel King, Vincent Hudson, Posey N. Smith, Zedekiah Merritt, Jefferson Glascock, Green McFarland, Ruth McPherson, Mr. Whitman, Matthew Barkley, James Eales, Judge Philips, Z. Merritt, Mr. Bebee, John Siler, H. W. Hamilton, John Wright, G. D. Hawkins, Henry Long, Wm. G. Johnson, Heath Jones, Mr. Turnball, Jeremiah Salor, James Buford, James Turley, John A. Wright, James L. Fisher, Daniel Brown, S. W. Mayhall, S. Smith, W. W. Beatty, Allen Brown, D. D. Dismukes, S. Porter, T. H. Purdom, H. Tapley. (RD) February 3, 1847, (CLK) John Ralls.

362) Second annual settlement of Sandi Fagan, adm. of the estate of Gerrard Fagan, dec. March term, 1847.

Monies Expended: Thornton Young, B.S. Ely, (RD) March 1, 1847, (CLK) John Ralls.

363) Second annual settlement of James Culbertson, adm. of the estate of Alexander Spotswood, dec. March term, 1847.

Monies Received: Witness for the State vs. Hudson.

Monies Expended: On July 3, 1846 to James Buford, On December 28, 1846 to R. B. Caldwell, On February 3, 1847 to G. C. Hays. (RD) March 2, 1847, (CLK) John Ralls.

364) First and final settlement of Chapel Carstarphen, adm. of the estate of George Carson, dec. April term, 1847.

Monies Expended: J. Sosey, John Tapley, Suel Hepbron, J. H. Humphreys, John Ralls, J. P. Ament. (RD) April 6, 1846, (CLK) John Ralls.

365) Second annual settlement of John B. Biggs, adm. of the estate of Robert Jamison, dec. May term, 1847.

Monies Expended: Est. of P. Kelsey, --- Watkins, Willes M. Jamison. (RD) May 3, 1847, (CLK) John Ralls.

366) Final settlement of Benjamin Ely, adm. of the estate of Thomas Ely, dec. May term, 1847.

Monies Expended: R. A. Daniel, James Leake, Isaac Ely, John Ralls. (RD) May 3, 1847, (CLK) John Ralls.

367) Final settlement of Ben A. Spalding, adm. of the estate of Abram Andrews, dec. May term, 1847.

Monies Expended: Robert Hagan, --- Jamison, A. W. Samls, R. Caldwell, -- Lacossett, J. Ralls. (RD) May 3, 1847, (CLK) John ralls.

368) Final settlement of Rapheal Leake, adm. of the estate of Charles Rohdes, dec. May term, 1847.

Monies Expended: H. Hagan, B. Ely, J.M. Smith, J. Francis, J. M. Smith, Mention of travel to St. Louis. (RD) May 3, 1847, (CLK) John Ralls.

369) Final settlement of George L. Hardy and Mary Blue, adm. of the estate of David Blue, dec. May term, 1847. Monies Expended: George S. Hardy, Joshua Wilson. (RD) May 3, 1847, (CLK) John Ralls.

370) Settlement of Elizabeth Weaver, adm. of the estate of Tilmon Weaver, dec. May term, 1847. Monies Expended: William Priest. (RD) May 3, 1847, (CLK) John Ralls.

371) First settlement of Samuel C. Woods, exr. of the estate of Isaac Ely, dec. May term, 1847. Monies Expended: Charles Rice, Ann Ely. (RD) May 3, 1847, (CLK) John Ralls.

372) First annual settlement of Richard Brashear adm. of the estate of Otho Brashear, dec. May term, 1847. Monies Received: Abram Liter, James Inlow, John M. Leake. Monies Expended: Charles Rice, Rosan I. Brashear, Dr. McElroy, Hays & Lampton, S. S. Anderson, W. O. Young, H. F. Wayland, R. Whitaker, John Tapley. (RD) May 4, 1847, (CLK) John Ralls.

373) Second annual settlement of James Buford, adm. of the estate of Leonard Porter, dec. Mary term, 1847. Monies Expended: --- Washington, --- Caldwell --- Glascock, --- Dismukes, P. H. Brown, R. W. Lyons, --- McMurty, --- Tapley, G. C. Hays, Y. I. Brown, --- Wright. (RD) May 4, 1847, (CLK) John Ralls.

374) Final settlement of Robert Baley, adm. of the estate of Charles Baley, dec. May term, 1847. Monies Expended: On January 23, 1844 to Charles Scanland for I. M. Iarboe, On June 29, 1844 to Hendley Haden, On June 29, 1844 to Peak & McKay, On March 1, 1844 to Nathan Haden, On February 1, 1845 to James Fuqua, On August 14, 1844 to A. & A. Buckner, On March 30, 1844 to C. F. Rogers, On January 3, 1845 to I. Scarce, On May 2, 1845 to J. Sosey, On February 1, 1845 to J. Creason. Insolvent notes: Rueben Hughert, Thomas P. Wilson. (RD) May 5, 1847, (CLK) John Ralls.

375) First annual settlement of William Cornet, adm. of the estate of Cheskey L. Mills, dec. May term, 1847. Monies Received: Land sold to T. B. Norton. Monies Expended: --- Buchanan. (RD) May 5, 1847, (CLK) John Ralls.

376) Final settlement of James Inlow, adm. of the estate of Peyton P. Wright, dec. August term, 1847. Monies Expended: On May 3, 1847 to Dudley V. Inlow, guardian; On August 3, 1847 to Dudley V. Inlow, guardian for Joseph H. Wright. (RD) August 3, 1847, (CLK) John Ralls.

377) Second annual settlement of Martin N. Jefferies, adm. of the estate of Joseph Jefferies, dec. August term, 1847.

Monies Received: --- Glascock.

Monies Expended: On August 1, 1846 to I. Glascock, On August 1, 1846 to A. Gilbert, On October 14, 1846 to E. N. Hascall, On March 1, 1846 to Gilbert, On February 1, 1846 for coffin, On February 1, 1846 for doctor bill for last sickness. (RD) August 3, 1847, (CLK) John Ralls, (DPY) E. W. Southworth.

378) Third annual settlement of Benjamin Ely, adm. of the estate of Aaron Ely, dec. August term, 1847.

No names given. (RD) August 3, 1847, (CLK) John Ralls, (DPY) E. W. Southworth.

379) Second annual settlement of Francis Conn, adm. of the estate of Mildred A. Conn, dec. August term, 1847.

Monies Expended: On September 29, 1846 to Joseph McGrew, as guardian for Rebbeca J. Williams; to Trammel Conn, David Clark, Abasalom Ellis, as guardian of E. Williams; to Tho. T. Williams; On October 5, 1846 to Tramel Conn; On November 1, 1845 to A. R. Maddox; On August 1, 1846 to R.B. Caldwell; On August 1, 1844 to John Tapley;On August 29, 1846 to Trammel Conn; On September 8, 1837 (sic) to John Cobb; On April 30, 1846 to Isaac Scarce; On November 1, 1845 to James Culbertson; In 1846 to Rebecca J. On September 29, 1846 to the guardian of Francis Williams and Mildred Ann Williams. (RD) August 3, 1847, (CLK) John Ralls, (DPY) E. W. Southworth.

380) Second annual settlement of Charles Rice, surviving exr. of the estate of THomas Hicklin, dec. August term, 1846.

No names given. (RD) August 4, 1847, (CLK) John Ralls, (DPY) E. W. Southworth.

381) Second annual settlement of William Newland, exr. of the estate of Mary McCleland, dec. August term, 1847.

Monies Expended: Akinson & McAser, R. B. Caldwell, to myself as guardian of Julia A. Miller. (RD) September 6, 1847, (CLK) John Ralls, (DPY) E. W. Southworth.

382) First annual settlement of William Settle, adm. of the estate of Thomas Settle, dec. August term, 1847.

Monies Received: Isaac Painter, Turner G. Priest, James Eales, Matthew McKenna, Benjamin Stinson.

Monies Expended: In September, 1846 to James D. Watson and Jas. Fuqua; On January 1, 1845 to Bengn. Stinson; On April 7, 1846 to Mary F. Winn; On July 26, 1847 to Dr. Hugh Meredith; On Janaury 23, 1845 to J. S. Buchanan; On October 12, 1846 to E. N. Hascall; On December 28, 1844 to Capt. Ralls and S. C. Northcut; In 1846 to John D. Slosson.

Insolvent Notes: James Eales. (RD) September 6, 1847, (CLK) John Ralls, (DPY) E. W. Southworth.

383) First annual settlement of Thomas Cleaver, exr. of the estate of Stephen Cleaver, dec. August term, 1847.

Notes Outstanding: Due May 13, 1846 from I.D. Wilson, Due

April 1, 1845 from Heath Jones; Due March 1, 1846 from Stephen Glascock; Due February 3, 1845 from John Ralls; Due July 12, 1847 from J. Briscoe; Due December 16, 1845 from Peter W. Pearce; Due September 9, 1841 from Granville Clayton; Due October 29, 1845 from Wm. B. Rogers; Due January 1, 1844 from E. & W. Spawn; Due December 21, 1845 from F. Glascock; Due January 1, 1846 from R. B. Caldwell; Due November 3, 1845 from E. Hopkins; Due January 1, 1846 from W. English; Due February 15, 1844 from H. Tapley; Due August 31, 1843 from H. Tapley; Due January 1, 1846 from H. Earley; Due March 10, 1846 from D. D. Dismuke; Due February 23, 1846 from J. S. Dimmitt; Due August 15, 1846 from R. Vermillion; Due October 1, 1845 from Wm. Caldwell; Due October 3, 1845 from Wm. Gerrard; Due January 1, 1842 from John Glascock; Due February 2, 1846 from Wm. Newland; Due January 1, 1846 from John Ralls; Due January 1, 1846 from James Dunkum; Due January 1, 1846 from Allen Brown; Due February 16, 1848 from George Rice; Due January 1, 1846 from Thomas Cleaver; Due January 1, 1844 from J. Glascock; Due January 21, 1845 from C. Northcut; Due January 1, 1845 from S. Cross; Due January 1, 1844 from S. Cross; Due from Thomas Winn (no date); Due November 6, 1842 from O. Glascock; Due December 1, 1841 from S. W. Mayhall; Due February 18, 1846 from Joel Ledford; Due September 1, 1846 from Thomas Cleaver; Due January 2, 1848 from A. Briscoe; Mary Cleaver (no date); Due August 3, 1847 from Grayson Dulin.

Monies Expended: G. C. Hays, Drs. Clayton & Strode, Dr. Peake, Reason Vermillion, Cash & Jones, Tate & Turnbull, J. R. McReynolds, J. D. Biggs, G. S. Thompson, Dabney Jones, H. S. Jackson, Mary Cleaver, William Jones, Anderson Briscoe, J. J. Cobb, Wm. and H. Cleaver. (RD) September 7, 1847, (CLK) John Ralls, (DPY) E. W. Southworth.

384) Second annual settlement of John C. Dawson, adm. of the estate of James Ferrill, dec. October term, 1847.

Monies Expended: L.I.T. McElroy, S. Anderson, J.J. Lyle, Dr. B. Kendrick, J. F. Hawkins. (RD) October 4, 1847, (CLK) John Ralls, (DPY) E. W. Southworth.

385) First annual settlement of Saml. G. Ewing, adm. of the estate of Walker Carter, dec. October term, 1847.

Monies Received: Wheat sold in St. Louis on April 13, 1847.

Monies Expended: James G. Glascock, Wm. Reed, Silvester Buchanan, James Glascock, S. B. Clermont, George Harrison, Wellman & Blackstone, Cily Weighers. (RD) October 4, 1847, (CLK) John Ralls, (DPY) E. W. Southworth.

386) Settlement of William Priest, adm. of the estate of William Bast, dec. November term, 1847.

Monies Expended: --- Coffman, Dr. Meredith, John M. Johnson, Bouris & Marquims, Barnet Gregory, Enoch Sims, William

Tumers, Thos. & Henderson Gregory, J. A. Henderson, Wm. Alford, Elizabeth Marcus, Wm. G. Dovor, Alr. McMurty. Insolvent Debts: A. W. Mills' note which cannot be made. John Ballard's note is insolvent and he left for Santafee. Joel Hudson has gone out of the country and Levi R. Dodd states that the note was paid to Bast. William Jenkins' account in insolvent and he has gone to Mexico. Jane White is insolvent. Perry Davis is in solvent and is not in the county. Thos W. Glascock is insolvent and lives in Shelby. Thos. S. Dodd is insolvent. (RD) November 1, 1847, (CLK) John Ralls, (DPY) E. W. Southworth.

387) Final settlement of Mary King and James King, adms. of the estate of Russell King dec. November term, 1847.

Monies Expended: Due October 26, 1844 to A. W. Perdom, Jackson & Wills, T. Cash, Peake & Strode, --- Brown. (RD) November 2, 1847, (CLK) John Ralls, (DPY) E. W. Southworth.

388) Second annual settlement of Wm. A. Shulse and Silas M. Rosser, adm. of the estate of Levi More, dec. November term, 1847.

Monies Expended: On May 3, 1847 payment was made to the Widow; On December 4, 1846 to Allen Alexander; On November 28, 1846 to Mark Shulse; On February 5, 1847 to William T. Bond; On December 4, 1846 to Wm. Little; On November 1, 1847 to Silas M. Rosser; On November 1, 1847 to Wm. A. Shulse. (RD) November 1, 1847, (CLK) John Ralls, (DPY) E. W. Southworth.

389) Fourth annual settlement of Alexander and Abraham Buford, exrs. of the estate of Abraham Buford, dec. November term, 1846.

Sale of Slaves: Sale of slave, James, about June 1, 1844 with interest until November 10,1847; Sale of slave, Thomas, about June 1, 1844 with interest until November 10, 1847, Sale of Scott, a slave, about June 17, 1844 with interest until November 10, 1847, Sale of slave, Emerson, on June 17, 1844 with interest until November 1, 1847.

Monies Expended: On November 4, 1844 to S. Hill, adm. of A. Hill; On January 18, 1844 to S. Hill, adm. of A. Hill; On November 23, 1844 to S. Hill, adm. of A. Hill; On February 11, 1845 to S. Hill, adm. of A. Hill; On July 7, 1844 to S. Hill, adm. of A. Hill; On April 10, 1845 to Hill, adm. of Hill; On February 3, 1845 to William McClune; On November 3, 1837 to D. Jones; On February 14, 1844 to --- McCune; On December --, 1841 to John Smith; On August 14, 1844 to Thos. S. Miller; On March 4, 1847 to J. Emerson, sr.; On May 14, 1845 to J. D. S. Dryden; On October 7, 1844 to John Tapley; On July 27, 1844 to J. S. Buchanan; On March 3, 1840 to Alexander McGaw; On May 4, 1844 to Joshua Brashears; On May 1, 1845 to J. Lyle; On April 4, 1842 to Thos. I. Rhodes; On November --, 1844 to W. S. McClune; On September 15, 1846 to

W. S. McClune; On September 25, 1844 to W. S. McClune; On October 2, 1844 to Thomas Priest; On December 27, 1844 to Uriel Wright; On December 6, 1845 to James Culbertson; On October 18, 1845 to Thos. Priest; On March 23, 1843 to Wm. H. Peaker; On November 4, 1844 to John J. Slosson; On October 3, 1842 to Thos. Buford; On October 7, 1844 to J. D. Tapley; On September 13, 1843 to Uriel Wright; On June 1, 1844 to J. Small; On April 4, 1842 on Abraham Buford's account; Expenses of Alex. Buford, of the administrators. (RD) November 10, 1847, (CLK) John Ralls, (DPY) E. W. Southworth.

390) Final settlement of William Stears, adm. of the estate of Holiday Stears, dec. December term, 1846. (sic)
No names given. (RD) December 7, 1846 (sic), (CLK) John Ralls.

391) Second annual settlement of James Glascock, adm. of the estate of Lucy J. Glascock, dec. December term, 1847.
No names given. (RD) December 6, 1847, (CLK) John Ralls, (DPY) E. W. Southworth.

392) Final settlement of Mahala Glascock, adm. of the estate of Thomas L. Glascock, dec. November term, 1847.
Monies Expended: John Ralls, Peter Elliott. (RD) December 7, 1847, (CLK) John Ralls, (DPY) E. W. Southworth.

393) First annual settlement of Samuel B. Caldwell and Elizabeth Robinson, adm. of the estate of Benjamin Robinson, dec. December term, 1847.
Monies expended: On December 4, 1846 to Albert Robinson; On December 4, 1846 to John Trimble; On January 5, 1847 to Wm. Tracy for coffin; On January 10, 1847 to J. P. Ament; On April 8, 1847 paid B. Robinson's note to C. Carstarphen; On December 23, 1846 to H. D. Sacossett; Payment to S. B. Caldwell, adm. for going to Kentucky on business; On March 12, 1846 to James Sneed; On October 27, 1847 to Drs. Clayton and Strode; On August 8, 1847 to William Robinson; On October 8, 1846 to Hays & Lampton; In 1847 to John M. Ayers; On February 10, 1847 to John Smith; On December 9, 19846 to A. Parker for crying sale.; In June, 1847 to B. Rogers. (RD) December 7, 1847, (CLK) John Ralls, (DPY) E. W. Southworth.

394) First annual settlement of Benjn. A. Spalding, public adm. and exofficio adm. of the estate of John M. Kelsey, dec. December term, 1847.
Monies Received: On November 7, 1846 received from the decease's account from Chapel Carstarphen, former adm. (RD) December 7, 1847, (CLK) John Ralls, (DPY) E. W. Southworth.

395) Second annual settlement of John Liter, exr. of the estate of John Litler, sr., dec. December term, 1847.
Monies Expended: Isaac Liter, Dudley Butler, Christian Liter, Abraham Liter, Ichabod Butler, Nathan Wheeler, John Brice, Adm. part of the legacy, James Campbell, Daniel

McAntire, (RD) December 7, 1847, (CLK) John Ralls, (DPY) E. W. Southworth.

396)   Second annual settlement of Isaac Searce, adm. of the estate of Robert Wright, dec. December term, 1847. Monies Received: S. K. Caldwell. Monies Expended: On May 12, 1846 to Mary J. Wright; On March 2, 1846 to S. W. Mayhall; On May 8, 1846 to G.C. Hays; On February 7, 1846 to R. W. Lyons; On February 7, 1846 to D. P. & N. Fike; On May 4, 1846 to G. Glascock; In July, 1846 to Mary J. Wright; On June 4, 1847 to A. Briscoe; On December 7, 1846 to larkin N. Wright; On November 8, 1847 to Mary J. Wright; On November 7, 1844 to Joseph P. Amment; Thomas Coke; James Culbertson; In May, 1846 to G. C. Hays and William Tracy. (RD) January 4, 1848, (CLK) William O. Young.

397)   First annual settlement of George G. Muldrow, adm. of the estate of Andrew Muldrow, dec. January term, 1848. Monies Received: Note of Charlotte Muldrow for the hire of slaves, Eliza, Richard and Robin for 1847. Note of W. T. Dubois for the hire of slave, Lucinda, for 1847. Note of Dr. Ferguson for the hire of slave, Martha, for 1847. Note of Benedict Dubois for the hire of slave, Mary, for 1847. Note on A. McElroy. Monies Expended: On November 27, 1846 to T. E. Hatcher; On November 27, 1846 to F. Hopson; On November 26, 1846 to T. M. Campbell; On January 4, 1847 to J. P. Rutter; On February 5, 1847 to --- Caldwell; On February 9, 1847 to J. H. Keith; On February 17, 1847 to Blue; On February 19, 1847 to J. Sosey; On october 1, 1847 to J. S. Crosthwait; On October 1, 1847 to A. G. Galleher; On October 1, 1847 to the Widow; In 1847 to John A. Steen; Payment a cap for boy, Nat; Cash paid to John Muldorw; Dr. McElroy; Wm. Dunn. (RD) January 4, 1848, (CLK) William O. Young.

398)   First annual settlement of William Gerard, jr., adm. of the estate of Alexander H. Gerard, dec. January term, 1848. Monies Expended: On February 19, 1847 to James S. Martin; On March 22, 1847 to James S. Martin; On May 4, 1847 to James S. Martin; In April, 1847 to Samuel O. Lyle; On May 4, 1847 to Geo. Scheroter; On April 30, 1847 to A. B. Asary; On May 12, 1847 to Wm. Greathouse; On May 12, 1847 to E. J. Hawkins; On June 10, 1847 to A. W. Lamb; On May 3, 1847 to J. J. T. McElroy; In May, 1847 to John M. Ayres; On November 30, 1846 to J. S. Buchanan. (RD) January 4, 1848, (CLK) Wm. O. Young.

399) First annual settlement of Wm. Gerard, jr., adm. of the estate of Joseph W. Gerard, dec. January term, 1847. Monies Expended: On June 10, 1847 to J. J. T. McElroy; On June 7, 1847 to H. Hendrix; On April 8, 1847 to A. Camp-

bell; On April 8, 1847 to S. S. Mulbry; On May 4, 1847 to Geo. Shroter; On May 12, 1847 to William Greathouse. (RD) January 4, 1848, (CLK) William O. Young.

400) First annual settlement of William Underwood and Sandie Fagan, adms. of the estate of Philip Myers, dec. February term, 1848.

Monies Received: Jeptha Thurman, Alvin Cartmell, Sandie Fagan, John C. Gatson.

Monies Expended: On May 3, 1847 to William Underwood; On February 4, 1848 to J. J. T. McElroy; On February 4, 1848 to H. G. Gallaher; On January 5, 1847 to H.D. Cossitt; On March 1, 1847 to Sandie Fagan; On July 23, 1847 to Martha Fagan; J. H. Keith. (RD) February 7, 1848, (CLK) William O. Young.

401) Settlement of Elizabeth Weaver, adm. of Tilman Weaver, dec. February term, 1848.

Monies Expended: William Priest. (RD) February 7, 1848, (CLK) William O. Young.

402) Third and final settlement of William Settle, adm. of the estate of Thomas Settle, dec. February term, 1848.

Monies Expended: J. S. Buchanan, S. C. Northcut, Matthew McKenna, --- Guluac, Wm. Stears, --- Ralls, E.W. Southworth. (RD) February 7, 1848, (CLK) William O. Young.

403) Final settlement of James Culbertson, adm. of the estate of Alexander W. Spotswood, dec. February term, 1848.

Monies Expended: On March 28, 1847 to Tyre A. Haden; On April 5, 1847 to Thos. A. Anderson; On April 5, 1847 to John Jamison; On July 22, 1847 to John Ralls; On October 4, 1847 to Joshua S. Ely; On December 8, 1847 to J. S. Buchanan. (RD) February 8, 1848, (CLK) Wm. O. Young.

404) Final settlement of William Cornet, adm. of the estate of Chesley Mills, dec. February term, 1848.

Monies Expended: On May --, 1844 to H. Meriedth; On May --, 1844 to B. T. Norton; On May 13, 1847 to Wm. Stephens; On February 5, 1848 to H. D. Lacossett; Paid J. S. Buchanan; On February 12, 1848 to James & Meredith; Paid John Ralls. and --- Lockwood. (RD) February 9, 1848, (CLK) William O. Young.

405) Final settlement of Drury Eads, exr. of the estate of Thomas Dooley, dec. February term, 1848.

Monies Expended: J. S. Buchanan. (RD) February 10, 1848, (CLK) Willia, O. Young.

406) Final settlement of James Hornback, adm. of the estate of Zephaniah Keith, dec. February term, 1848.

Monies Expended: J. S. Buchanan, Mr. Harris, John Ralls, Wm. O. Young. (RD) February 11, 1848, (CLK) Wm. O. Young.

407) Fourth annual settlement of Joshua Gentry, adm. of the estate of Rodes Gentry, dec. February term, 1848.

Monies Expended: G. Porter; Moffet, Moffett, Hans & Co.; John Ralls. (RD) February 11, 1848, (CLK) William O. Young.

59

408) First annual settlement of Fountain Kenney, adm. of the estate of John Kennedy, dec. February term, 1848.
Monies Received: Sale bill dated February 26, 1847 and February 17, 1847.
Monies Expended: On January 17, 1847 to S. S. Anderson for coffin; On On February 29, 1848 paid J. J. T. McElroy, Richard M. Leake, William Snider, Stephen T. Elliott, George S. Hardy, John J. Lyle, John M. Calhoun, James Leake, John Ralls. (RD) March 7, 1848, (CLK) William O. Young.
409) Second annual settlement of Bayles G. Rector, adm. of the estate of Volentine P. Matson, dec. April term, 1848.
Monies Recieved: On May 5, 1847 from G. R. Green.
Monies Expended: J. S. Buchanan, James Fuqua, John Ralls, C. Carstarphen, S. Brothers, S.M. Creason, John F. Fletcher, Thomas S. McAfee, N. Dye, S. K. Caldwell, S. K. Hakins, Wm. H. Peake. (RD) April 3, 1848, (CLK) William O. Young.
410) First annual settlement of Robert Hagan, adm. of the estate of Butler W. Brown, dec. April term, 1848.
Monies Expended: James Alexander, T. P. Norton, Paid for travel getting a witness from Shelby Co. (RD) May 1, 1848, (CLK) William O. Young.
411) Third and final settlement of Sandie Fagan, adm. of the estate of Gerard Fagan, dec. May term, 1848.
Monies Expended: T. M. Campbell, P. Myers, Wm. Martin, Geo. G. Muldrow, Joshua Ely, jr., H. D. LaCossitt, T. Young, C. Carstarphen, Wm. O. Young, John Ralls, S. K. Caldwell. (RD) May 1, 1848, (CLK) William O. Young.
412) Second annual settlement of Mary Ann Winn, adm. of the estate of Thos. Winn, dec. May term, 1848.
Monies Expended: William Stears, N. Gilbert, Clark Finch, Dr. T. Rodes, Petter C. Settles, J. O. Winn, B. G. Rector, Estate of Volentine Matson, dec. (RD) May 1, 1848, (CLK) Wm. O. Young.
413) First annual settlement of Hiram W. Glascock, adm. of the estate of Eliza Rhodes, dec. May term, 1848.
Monies Expended: William Tracy, John K. Hawkins, French Glascock, Grayson Dulin, James Small, Jacob Saffell, Hays & Herlinger, Hays & Lampton, Jesse Heldreth, John Tracy, Dr. R. B. Bronaugh (gone to Mexico, dead and insolvent), Pierce & Kennedy, Wm. Priest, H. Brown. (RD) May 1, 148, (CLK) Wm. O. Young.
414) First annual settlement of S. R. Flowerree, adm. of the estate of Margaret Glascock, dec. May term, 1848.
Notes Due: One note dated November 30, 1836 on K. M. Glascock, One note dated December 25, 1837 on K.M. Glascock, One note dated January 1, 1839 on K. M. Glascock, On note dated December 25, 1839 on K. M. Glascock, One note dated December 28, 1837 on B. P. Glascock, One note dated April 1, 1840 on B. P. Glascock, One note dated December 28, 1836 on

E. H. Glascock, One note dated August 11, 1838 on E.H. Glascock, One note on D. M. Glascock dated December 1, 1840, One note on J. S. Sanders dated February 3, 1840, One note on Eliza Glascock dated December 14, 1840, Sale due February 28, 1846. (RD) May 1, 1848, (CLK) Wm. O. Young.

415) Third and final settlement of Lovel Rouse, adm. of the estate of George Rouse, dec. May term, 1848.

Monies Expended: Alen Rouse, J. S. Buchanan, E.W. Southworth, Wm. O. Young.

Insolvent Notes: Note on E. B. Hall dated December 22, 1840; Note on Saml. Haynes dated March 26, 1845 (Charged on inventory).

416) First annual settlement of Joel Finks, adm. of the estate of Thomas R. Chedester, dec. May term, 1848.

Monies Expended: Lewis S. Anderson, H. D. Lacoseitt, Hurt Yager, John Ralls, Wm. O. Young. Mention of trip to Hannibal. (RD) May 2, 1848, (CLK) Wm. O. Young.

417) First annual settlement of John D. Smith and Bartlet G. White, exrs. of the last will and testament of Stephen McPherson, dec. May term, 1848.

Monies Received: William Collins, W. M. Halsey, Allen Dodd, Wm. Allen, Robert Rudesell, Robert Buchanan, William Hutchison.

Monies Expended: --- Kercheval, J. Hornback, B.C. Keith, M. H. Keith, J. H. Keith, T. H. Davis, James Hornback, W. O. Young, --- Jamison, Zephaniah Keith, S. W. Watkins. (RD) May 2, 1848, (CLK) Wm. O. Young.

418) Second annual settlement of Richard M. Brashear, adm. of the estate of Otho Brashear, dec. May adjourned term, 1848.

Monies Expended: Charles Rice, Wm. Leake, R. M. Leake, Saml. K. Caldwell, Elsea Allison. (RD) June 5, 1848, (CLK) Wm. O. Young.

419) Annual settlement of Branch Hatcher, adm. of the estate of S. P. Cook, dec. May term, 1848.

Monies Expended: Boarding and clothing for Elizabeth, Mary Jane and Ann Eliza Cook for 27 months. Settlement with E. Cook. (RD June 6, 1858, (CLK) Wm. O. Young.

420) First annual settlement of Fountain Kenney, surviving partner of Thomas P. Norton, dec. June term, 1848.

Monies Expended: On October 5, 1847 to B. & I. Ely; On October 8, 1847 to James Wood, On October 29, 1847 to Joel Finks; On October 29, 1847 to Urial Rouse; On November 1, 1847 to S. Matthews; Paid T. P. Norton; Paid W. McFarlin; On December 22, 1847 to T. P. Norton; Paid Uriel Rouse; Paid Joel A. Finks; On February 8, 1848 made a trip to Hannibal; Paid on February 19, 1828 W. McFarland, Thomas Iman, Robert Briggs, Thomas Hagan, Uriel Rouse, W. H. Vardeman, Benjamin Ely, Frederic Lane, Robert Hagan, Moses Hawkins, Stephen T.

Elliott, James S. Ledford, John Matthews, Joel A. Finks,
Thomas I. Ellis, John Mastin, Speed Ely, R. S. Warren, James
T. Hagan, R. S. Warren, Wm. B. Norton, Lakeman & Sunderland,
Robert Spalding, Levi Keithley, Peter Shulse, J.P. Richards,
John McReynolds, B. King, Eliza E. Richmond, Benj. A. Spal-
ding. (RD) June 6, 1848, (CLK) William O. Young.
421)   First annual settlement of John I. Sinklear, adm.
of the estate of James Sneed, dec. May term, 1848.
Monies Expended: On May 17, 1848 to John P. B. Forman;
On April 5, 1847 to T. Rodes; On February 24, 1847 to N. P.
Hornback; In 1847 to Hedgeman Wilson, jr.; On March 24, 1847
to J. P. B. Forman; On March 2, 1847 to William Maddox; On
March 2, 1847 to J. S. Buchanan. (RD) June 6, 1848, (CLK)
William O. Young.
422) First annual settlement of Michael Jones, adm. of
the estate of Geo. W. Gillespie, dec.   May term, 1848.
Monies Received. On October 7, 1845 note on E. A.
Hascall.
Monies Expended: On March 20, 1848 articles selected by
the Widow; On August 3, 1837 the demand of Samuel Smith; On
February 6, 1847 to J. Dunkum; On June 17, 1847 to J.C. Wel-
born; On June 17, 1847 to Adam Mace; On October 6, 1847 to
H. F. Inlow; On November 5, 1846 to Tate & Turnbull; On Oct-
ober 24, 1846 to Deven & Lewellen; On June 17, 1847 to C. J.
Gillespie; On August 7, 1847 to T. Cash; On May 10, 1847 to
R. Vermillion; On January 30, 1845 to J. A. Wright; On Sep-
tember 25, 1845 to Murray & Peck. (RD) June 6, 1848, (CLK)
Wm. O. Young.
423) First annual settlement of James T. Hagan, adm. of
the estate of Cornelius N. Lynch, dec. May term, 1848.
Monies Received: Hire of slaves, Charlotte and two chil-
dren in September, 1847. Hire of slave, Warren, in 1847.
Monies Expended: John Kenney: Reuben Reddish; On January
13, 1848 to J. B. Kendrick; On August 20, 1847 to Hamilton
Boony; On July 3, 1848 to J. A. Spalding; On May 31, 1848 to
James Leake; On March 12, 1848 to George L. Hardy; On July
3, 1847 to Allen Bast; On July 15, 1847 to James Cooper; On
August --, 1847 to Speed Ely; On January 3, 1848 to R. B.
Calddwell; On October 7, 1847 to H. D. Lacossett; On July
18, 1847 to S. S. Anderson; On June 29, 1847 to John Blue;
On May 27, 1847 to J. B. Gore for --- Buchanan; On April 25,
1848 to J. J. I. McElroy; On July 3, 1848 to J. Ralls and E.
W. Southworth; On July --, 1847 clothing for negro boy, Warren; In 1847 to correct an error in J. A. Spalding's note.
(RD) July 3, 1848, (CLK) William O. Young.
424) First annual settlement of B. A. Spalding, public
administrator, of the estate of Thomas Brown, dec. August
term, 1848.
No names given. (RD) August 6, 1848, (CLK) Wm. O. Young.

425) Third and final settlement of Francis Conn, adm. of the estate of Mildred Ann Conn, dec. August term, 1848. Monies Expended: --- Wiley, --- Martin, ---Suallins, --- Collins, R. C. Caldwell, Buchanan & Eastin, Wm. O. Young. (RD) August 8, 1848, (CLK) Wm. O. Young.

426) Third annual settlement of Chs. Rice, surviving executor of the estate of Thomas Hicklin, dec. August term, 1848. Monies Expended: On August 11, 1847 to John Tapley; On May 9, 1848 to J. H. Humphreys, On March 20, 1848 to R. B. Caldwell; In 1847 to Young & Perry. (RD) August 8, 1848, (CLK) Wm. O. Young.

427) Fourth and final settlement of Benjamin Ely, adm. of the estate of Aaron Ely, dec. August term, 1848. Monies Expended: Simpson Smith, Thomas Sipps, Benjamin Kendrick, Robert Snider, Estate of James Ferrill. (RD) August 9, 1848, (CLK) Wm. O. Young.

428) First annual settlement of William R. Campbell, adm. of the estate of Wm. I. McElroy, dec. August term, 1848. Monies Expended: On July 22, 1847 to J. S. Buchanan, On December --, 1847 to R. B. Caldwell; On July 15, 1847 to John A. Quarles; On August 6, 1847 to Geo. Biggers. (RD) August 9, 1848, (CLK) Wm. O. Young.

429) Third and final settlement of James Buford, adm. of the estate of Leonard Porter, dec. August term, 1848. Monies Received: Due on March 1, 1849 from Geo. C. Hays for the rent of land; Due on March, 1, 1849 from Nelson Fike and J. T. Benzendine for the rent of land; Due from Saffell and Kennedy for the rent of land in 1847. Monies Expended: J. S. Buchanan, Sam. W. Mayhall, R. B. Caldwell, John Ralls, Wm. O. Young, Thos. A. Purdom. (RD) August 9, 1848, (CLK) Wm. O. Young.

430) Third annual settlement of Martin B. Jefferies, adm. of the estate of Joseph Jefferies, dec. August term, 1848. Monies Expended: On December 6, 1847 to J. P. Ament; On August 26, 1843 to E. W. Hascall; T. Wilson. (CLK) William O. Young, (RD) August 10, 1848.

431) First annual settlement of Hanceford Brown, adm. of the estate of Daniel Brown, dec. August term, 1848. Monies Received: Wilkinson Cranford; Hire of negro boy to December 25, 1847. Monies Expended: H. D. LaGosett, Glascock & Tracy, Wm. Tracy, N. H. Buckner, D. C. Tuttle, G. C. hays, Hays & Lampton, Hays & Gore, B.G. Rector, D. Willock, Clayton & Strode, Hawkins & Saffel. (RD) August 10, 1848, (CLK) Wm. O. Young.

432) Second annual settlement of Thomas Cleaver, exr. of the estate of Stephen Cleaver, dec. September term, 1848.

Monies Received: On Septemer 10, 1847 to J. Fisher; On October 1, 1847 from James Culbertson; On October 5, 1847 from Charles Scanland; On December 22, 1847 from Wm. Gerard; February 1, 1848 from H. Brown; On April 8, 1848 from G. Rice; On June 5, 1848 from H. Northcut; From June 6, 1848 from George Rice; On June 21, 1848 from Wm. H. Vardeman; On August 1, 1848 from D. Dismukes; Cash from Henry Early; Wm. Splawn; A. Briscoe; R. & J. K. Caldwell; John Coleman.

Monies Expended: Mary Cleaver, A. Briscoe, J. A. Cobb, William Jones. (RD) September 4, 1848, (CLK) Wm. O. Young.

433) First annual settlement of Allen Rouse, adm. of the estate of Jonathan Hill, dec. September term, 1848.

Monies Received: Sale bill of personal property filed October 4, 1848 (?) (sic).

Monies Expended: On September 1, 1848 to J. J. Noyes; On August --, 1847 to P. S. James; On November 1, 1847 to ; On September 15, 1847 to J. Fudge and Lovel Rouse; On September --, 1847 to -- Buchanan; On September 4, 1848 to E.W. Southworth. (RD) September 4, 1848, (CLK) Wm. O. Young.

434) First annual settlement of Samuel Smith, adm. of the estate of Thomas Purdom, dec. August term, 1848.

Monies Received: Geo. S. Martin.

Monies Expended: Job Harlinger, Charles B. Clark, John Tracy, N. Gilbert, H. Brown, Estate of Robert M'Kay, J. P. Allen, H. N. Buford, William Fisher, C. F. Clayton. (RD) September 5, 1848, (CLK) William O. Young.

435) Second annual settlement of Jonathan Abbay, jr., exr. of the estate of Jonathan Abbay, sr., dec. October term, 1848.

Monies Expended: H. Monefee, J. Fagan, Wm. Dubois, James Abbay, Louisa Sexton, John R. Hall, Wm. C. and J. Abbay, J. J. McElroy, --- Chowning, J. Quinn, In August, 1847 to B. S. Ely, In 1848 to S. K. Caldwell, In 1848 to Wm. O. Young, In 1848 to Alvin Menefee. (RD) October 2, 1848, (CLK) William O. Young.

436) First annual settlement of James Ely and Joshua Ely, adms. of the estate of Benjamin Ely, dec. November term, 1848.

Monies Received: Note on Sarah Sun due June 4, 1845; Note on John Gatson; Note on Thos. & James Ely due November 25, 1847; Claim allowed in the Pike County Court against Betty Perry or estate dated January 6, 1846; Note on R. Cocket and D. Rice due October 25, 1848; Note on A. Menefee due January 4, 1848; Note on J. C. Coliver due January 4, 1848; Note on J. H. Keith due January 4, 1848; Note on Sandie Fagan due January 4, 1848; Note on N. Allison due January 12, 1848; Note on N. Allison due January 13, 1848; Note on Wm. Biggers due November 19, 1847.

Monies Expended: On September 8, 1847 to H. de LaCossit;

On October 4, 1847 to Wm. O. Young; On October 19, 1847 to J. S. Crosthwait; On November 1, 1847 to R. B. Caldwell; In September, 1848 to John Hurley'On November 4, 1848 to Johnson Barnard; Cash paid to James Ely; J. Hurley; Thos. Ely. (RD) November 6, 1848, (CLK) William O. Young.

437) Final settlement of William A. Shulse and Silas M. Rosser, adms. of the estate of Levi Moler, dec. November term, 1848.

Monies Expended: Buchanan & Easton, Wm. A. Shulse, E. W. Southworth, William O. Young. (RD) November 6, 1848, (CLK) William O. Young.

438) Second annual settlement of William Priest, adm. of the estate of William Bast, dec. November term, 1848.

No names given. (RD) November 6, 1848, (CLK) William O. Young.

439) Fifth and last settlement of Abraham and Alexander Buford, adms. of the estate of Abraham Buford, sr., dec. November term, 1848.

Monies Received: Sale of the slave, Charles, to James Culbertson; Sale of two slaves, ages seven and ten, named Joe and Miles to J. Johnson; Negro woman, Rhodes, and three children, Jeff, Rueben, and Jane, are given the to Widow Mary Buford as agreeable to the terms of the will.

Monies Expended: On November 7, 1848 to Uriel Wright; On November 3, 1848 to Anderson & Dryden; On November 7, 1848 to H. Brown; On February 11, 1848 to Thomas Cleaver; On November 10, 1847 to Saml. H. Hill; On February 1, 1847 to S. Davis; On December 10, 1847 to Wm. S. M'Cune; On November 7, 1848 to J. S. Buchanan. (RD) November 7, 1848, (CLK) Wm. O. Young.

440) Third and final settlement of John C. Dawson, adm. of the estate of James Ferrill, dec. November term, 1848.

Monies Expended: John Ralls, Wm. O. Young, (RD) November 8, 1848, (CLK) Wm. O. Young.

441) Second annual settlement of Samuel G. Ewing, exr. of the estate of Walker Carter, dec. November term, 1848.

Monies Expended: Saml. G. Ewing, J. C. Welborn, William Reed. (RD) November 8, 1848, (CLK) Wm. O. Young.

442) Final settlement of John R. Floweree, adm. of the estate of Margaret Glascock, dec. November term, 1848.

Monies Received: Note of K. M. Glascock due November 30, 1836; Note on K. M. Glascock due January 1, 1839; Note on K. M. Glascock due December 25, 1839; Note on B. P. Glascock due December 28, 1837; Note on B. P. Glascock due April 18, 1840; Note on E. H. Glascock due December 28, 1836; Note on E. H. Glascock on April 18, 1837; Note on D. M. Glascock due December 1, 1840; Note on John J. Sanders due February 3, 1840; Note on Eliza Glascock due December 14, 1840; Cash from James Riggs on October 1, 1845; From Thomas Massie on

March 11, 1848; From George C. Lighte on May 1, 1846; From M. McMurty on November 1, 1847; Note on Reddin & Roberts dated April 1, 1846; Note on Isaac Reddin due December 1, 1846; Note on Rob. Massie due March 1,1849; From S. Smith on November 1, 1846.

Monies Expended: On July 29, 1844 to Saml. J. Harrison; On January 1, 1844 to to Wm. Ramsay; On January 28, 1845 to Dr. Jett; On January 1, 1845 to Dr. Tyre Rodes; On December 1, 1844 to J. S. Buchanan; On December 4, 1847 to John R. Floweree; On March 11, 1848 to Thomas Massie; On May 26, 1847 to the sheriff of Shelby Co.; On October 1, 1845 to Mr. Riggs; On November 28, 1848 to Buchanan & Easten; On November 17, 1848 to John Ralls; K. M. Glascock's account; Note returned on Isaac Reddin and Wm. K. Roberts; Obligation returned on Robert Bronaugh. (RD) November 18, 1848, (CLK) Wm. O. Young.

442) Second annual settlement of Samuel B. Caldwell and Elizabeth Robinson, adms. of the estate of Benjamin Robinson, dec. December term, 1848.

Monies Expended: Elizabeth Robinson, Benjamin Robinson, Hedgman Willson as guardian of William J. Robinson; Judgement in favor of John Hagar; C. Carstarphen; S. Craig; Elizabeth Robinson as guardian for Mary Robinson; Samuel Caldwell as guardian for Alphonso and John Robinson. (RD) December 5, 1848, (CLK) Wm. O. Young.

443) Final settlement of James Culbertson, adm. of the estate of Asa Glascock, dec. August adjourned term, 1848.

Monies Received: John Ralls; From Samuel Smith for the rent of the slave, Mead, for 1846; Charles Kennedy; John K. Hawkins; George Glascock; Eliza Glascock; Spencer Glascock; Allen N. Brown; Jefferson Glascock; William C. Wright; Jacob Saffel; Chapel Carstarphen; Leroy Hatchett; Hire of slaves, Bob and Judah, for part of 1847; Sale of slaves, Tobi, Bob, and Judah; French Glascock, jr.; Leroy Glascock.

Monies Expended: Stephen Glascock's bond dated January 11, 1819; Stephen Glascock's bond dated March 6, 1819; S. Glascock's bond dated August 3, 1836; Stephen Glascock's demand dated February 9, 1848; George C. Hays; Wm. H. Peake; Spencer Glascock for difference in slaves on July 16, 1846; Paid to --- Ballthrope on December 28, 1846; James Smith; Cash & English; John Jamison; John Byers; Martin Jefferies; James C. Lampton's demand paid on March 27, 1847; --- Hays as guardian for Ann Glascock; Edward G. Pratt; --- Scarce; Henny Robinson; James Glascock; Thos. C. Thompson; Allen Brown; John M. Floweree; Carty Wells; E. W. Southworth; John Glascock; Hiram Glascock; John Krigbaum; Wm. E. Harris; Glover & Campbell; Luke W. Watkins; S. W. Mayhall; Wm. Fuqua; James Garrish; Robert B. Caldwell; H. Wilson; S.K. Caldwell. (RD) December 5, 1848, (CLK) Wm. O. Young.

444) Third and final settlement of John Liter, exr. of the estate of John Liter, dec. November adjourned term, 1848.

Monies Expended: Estate of Elijah Brice; Samuel Brice; John Ralls; Wm. O. Young; J.P. Ament. (RD) January 1, 1849, (CLK) Wm. O. Young.

445) First annual settlement of Alexander Cause, adm. of the estate of James Flannery, dec. January term, 1849.

Monies Expended: On August 7, 1848 to J. S. Buchanan; On December --, 1848 to Wm. O. Young; On December 23, 1848 to A. F. Wayland; John H. Leake; Wm. O. Young; J.J.T. McElroy. (RD) January 1, 1849, (CLK) Wm. O. Young.

446) First annual settlement of Benj. A. Spalding, adm. of James Lee, dec. January term, 1849.

Monies Expended: --- McGee; Mrs. Magees; --- Leake; Mention of travel to Palmyra, Hannibal, London, Shelby Co.; --- Muldrow; William Martin.(RD) January 1, 1840, (CLK) William O. Young.

447) Settlement of Thomas Clark, adm. of the estate of Charles Fuqua, dec. November adjourned term, 1848.

Monies Received: Christian Slatery, T. Conn. (RD) January 1, 1849, (CLK) Wm. O. Young.

448) Second annual settlement of Ben A. Spalding, adm. of the estate of John M. Kelcy, dec. January term, 1849.

Monies Expended: R. Hagan; Mention of travel to Shelbyville and London; Taxes paid in Shelby Co. (RD) january 2, 1849, (CLK) Wm. O. Young.

449) Second annual settlement of George G. Muldrow, adm. of the estate of Andrew Muldrow, dec. January term, 1849.

Monies Received: Note on Charlotte Muldrow for the hire of the slaves, Richard, Eliza, Robert and Mary with two children; Note on Johnson Barnard for the hire of the slave, Ailsey and one child; Chapman Hitzer.

Monies Expended: On January 24, 1848 to John Muldrow; On March 7, 1848 to Wm. S. McCune assignee of --- Dubois; On January 22, 1848 to --- Thurman; On May 22,1848 to --- Thurman; On March 10, 1848 to B. Edellin; On February 19, 1848 to --- Southan; On December --, 1848 to the Widow; On January 24, 1848 to J.J. T. McElroy; On February 12, 1848 to R. B. Goodwin; On February 21, 1848 to Joshua Ely; On February 24, 1848 to J. Abbay, trustee of J. Henley; On March 6, 1848 to Robert Irvin; On March 6, 1848 to Jacob Welby; On February 1, 1848 to J. Barnard; On September 4, 1848 to Wm. O. Young and J. Ralls; On November 1, 1848 to Durbin Jones; On December 7, 1848 to Will Dunn; On December 7, 1848 to M. W. McCormic; On December 14, 1848 to Wm. T. Dubois; On December 17, 1848 to Margaret E. Muldrow; On August 19, 1848 to G. G. Muldrow and E. W. Southworth. (RD) January 1, 1849, (CLK) Wm. O. Young.

450) First annual settlement of Gilbert J. Thompson and William P. Tapley, adms. of the estate of Hannah Tapley, dec. February term, 1849.

Monies Expended: On February 10, 1848 to Wm. P. Tapley; On March 8, 1848 to Miss Sally Mase; On May 1, 1848 to R. B. Caldwell; On February 1, 1848 to J. S. Buchanan; On January 27, 1848 to Stark & Martin; On July 3, 1848 to G. J. Thompson; On September 22, 1848 to Wm. P. Tapley; On September 18, 1848 to E. Hudson; On February 2, 1849 to Wm. O. Young; On February 2, 1849 to R. Caldwell; On February 2, 1849 to Tate & Turnbull; On February 2, 1849 to G. C. Hays; On February 2, 1849 to Wm. Tracy; On Febryary 2, 1849 to Cash & Jones. (RD) February 5, 1849, (CLK) Wm. O. Young.

451) Second annual settlement of William Underwood and Sandie Fagan, adm. of the estate of Philip Myers, dec. March term, 1849.

Monies Expended: D. E. Rice; Martha Myers; Eli W. Southworth, William Underwood. (RD) March 6, 1849, (CLK) Wm. O. Young.

452) Second annual settlement of Samuel B. Vardeman and William H. Vardeman, dec. February adjourned term, 1849.

Monies Expended: J. B. Vardeman; On October 9, 1843 to J. S. Davis; On October 3, 1842 to Lewis Tracy; On October 7, 1844 to Dr. Jno. Hascall; On August 13, 1842 to Joseph P. Ament; On January 21, 1843 to Simon Davis; On January 21, 1841 to English & Cash; On June 2, 1845 to John Jamison; On August 12, 1842 to Wm. T. Bond, agent for J. Elliott; On June 15, 1848 to J. P Ament. (RD) April 2, 1849, (CLK) Wm. O. Young.

453) First annual settlement of Thomas Cleaver, adm. of the estate of John Tapley, dec. February adjourned term, 1849.

Notes Due: On William Newland due March 2, 1846; On John Brice due April 19, 1847; On William Treadway due February 11, 1847; On John Ralls due May 6, 1845; On McElory & Tapley due March 23, 1847; On William O. Young due April 8, 1845; On Pleasant Cox due November 1, 1841; On George Glascock due April 19, 1847; On Charles Glascock due January 22, 1844; On Joseph Hardy due November 5, 1846; On George C. Jefferies due June 3, 1846; On Robert B. Caldwell due December 1,1847; On Abner Smith on March 23, 1847; On Richd. M. Leake due October 18, 1846; On John Hagan due March 24, 1847; On Allen Brown due January 27, 1947; On John Seely due June 28, 1845; On Abraham Liter due September 17, 1845; On James Kerr on November 17, 1846; On Richard M. Brashear due October 6, 1847; On J. J. T. McElroy due May 4, 1847; On Isaac Liter due January 2, 1847; On Benjamin Ely due July 7, 1847; On Walter M. Quie due May 22, 1847; On George Ledford on September 25, 1843; On E. Allison due January 23, 1847; On J.J.

McElroy due January 20, 1847; On Matthew Smith due January 9, 1844; Eliza Caldwell due November 3, 1845; On Matthew Smith due January 1, 1844; On William S. Tipton due September 15, 1847; On John Brice due April 19, 1847; On Andrew Scott due January 16, 1847; Jeptha S. Crosthwaith due November 11, 1846; On John A. Woods due May 10, 1846; On J. J. T. McEroy due October 26, 1847; On J. S Ely due April 7, 1847; On Joseph Hardy due February 5, 1847; On Amos Ellis due September 22, 1846; On Saml. C. Woods due October 14, 1847; On John Ralls due December 30, 1846; On Stephen Glascock due April 2, 1847; On William C. Splawn due April 3, 1846; On David Griffin due February 9, 1847; On Jas. H. Humphrey with no date; On Charles Rice due March 9,1844; On Rich. M. Leake due January 2, 1844.

Monies Expended: William Tracy, R.B. Caldwell, J. Sosey, G. C. Hays, Widow Eliza Tapley, Jas. Culbertson, Geo. Rice, Jno. D. Biggs, J. W. Ellis, Wm. Boyd, Rich. M. Leake. (RD) April 2, 1849, (CLK) Wm. O. Young.

454) Settlement of Charles Williamson, adm. of the estate of James C. Shaw, dec. January term, 1849.

Monies Received: Bond on William Crawford due March 10, 1851; Note on Amos Hill and William Crawford due 6th of August; On receipt on William S. Ely for note on George and Alfred Shaver.

Monies Expended: John S. Thompson, Saml. Smith. (RD) April 2, 1849, (CLK) Wm. O. Young.

455) Fifth annual settlement of Joshua Gentry, adm. of the estate of Rodes Gentry, dec. February adjourned term, 1849.

Monies Expended: Glover & Campbell, Wm. B. Philips. (RD) April 3, 1849, (CLK) Wm. O. Young.

456) Settlement by Fountain Kenney and Wm. B. Norton, adm. of the estate of Thomas P. Norton, dec.

Monies Expended: On April 1, 1848 to Hurt Yager; On April 2, 1848 to George S. Hardy; On April 3, 1848 to George S. Hardy; On July 4, 1848 and July 15, 1848 to H. D. Lacossitt; On July 5, 1848 and July 26, 1848 to N. Fuqua; On July 26, 1848 to J. D. Adkins; On August 8, 1848 and August 9, 1848 to T. Bell; On August 28, 1848 to Joshua W. Ennis; On November 5, 1848 and November 6, 1848 to Ben Davis; On December 1, 1848 to A. Curts; On December 1, 1848 to B. B. King; On December 1, 1848 to see R. W. Moss; On December 1, 1848 to G. W. Barker; On August 12, 1848 to Henny Smesler; On September 4, 1848 to William C. Broughton; On October 14, 1848 to A. M. William; On October 14, 1848 to Geo. Settle; On October 14, 1848 to William Little; On October 14, 1848 to William Tipton; On October 13, 1848 to Mary Kelby; On October 13, 1848 to John Morris; On October 20, 1848 to Robert B. Caldwell; On December 4, 1848 to John McReynolds; on Jan-

uary 5, 1849 to Wm. O. Young; On January 3, 1849 to A. C.
On February 16, 1849 to Mary Blue; On February 17, 1849 to
Benj. A. Spalding; On February 23, 1849 to Elnathan Wicke;
On March 9, 1849 to Richard Warren; On March 9, 1849 to Al-
fred Alexander; On March 9, 1849 to Charles M. Asher; On
March 9, 1849 to Jacob Coonts; On March 6, 1849 to John W.
Lewellen; On March 29, 1849 to Hugh Emison; On March 29,
1849 to Mr. Hurley; Paid James Culbertson; Paid Robert Spal-
ding, sr.; On April 2, 1849 to Robert Hagar; Mention of tra-
vel to Hannibal and Palmyra; Mention of surveying in Shelby
Co. (RD) April 3, 1849, (CLK) Wm. Young.

457)   Second annual settlement of Fountain Kenney, adm.
of the estate of John Kenney, dec.
     Monies Expended: Hurt Yager; C. Carstarphen; On March
18, 1848 to Joseph Henderson; On March 27, 1848 to John
Jamison; In April, 1848 to Jas. T. Hager; On May 26, 1848 to
James Leake; On July 15, 1848 to H. D. Cossitt; Paid S. W.
Watkins; On September 1, 1848 trip to St. Louis regarding
Taylor's note; On July 11, 1848 and July 15, 1848 trip to
Palmyra to consult with Glover; Paid John Blue, John Shuck,
David O'Brien, J. J. T. McElroy, John Jamison, Mr. Liter
(RD) April 3, 1849, (CLK) William O. Young.

458)   Second annual settlement of William Gerrard, jr.
adm. of the estate of Alexander H. Gerrard, dec. May term,
1849.
     No names given. (RD) May 7, 1849 (CLK) William O. Young.

459)   Second annual settlement of William Gerrard, jr.
adm. for the estate of Joseph W Gerrard, dec. May term,
1849.
     Monies Expended: J. Hardy; William O. Young; J.S. Martin.
(RD) May 7, 1849, (CLK) Wm. O. Young.

460)   Second annual settlement of Hiram W. Glascock, adm.
of the estate of Eliza Rhodes, dec. May term 1849.
     Monies Expended: William Young D. W. H. Peake, James
Culbertson J. R. Smith, --- Naylor, Eliza Rodes (sic). (RD)
May 7, 1849, (CLK) Wm. O. Young.

461)   Second annual settlement of John G. Sinklear, adm.
of the estate of James Sneed, dec. May term, 1849.
     Monies Expended: Robert Briggs Dr. T. Rhodes. (RD) May
7, 1849, (CLK) Wm. Young

462)   Third annual settlement of Richard. M. Brashear,
adm. of the estate of Otho Brashear, dec. May term, 1849.
     Monies Expended: R. B. Caldwell, Wm. O. Young, J. S.
Buchanan, William A. Masson. (RD) May 7, 1849, (CLK) Wm. O.
Young.

463)   First annual settlement of E. C. and L. H. Redman,
adms. of the estate of Richard Redman, dec.
     Monies Expended: --- Spalding. (RD) May 7, 1849, (CLK)
Wm. O. Young.

464) First annual settlement of Hurt Yager, adm. of the estate of Lawson Berry, dec. May term, 1849.

No names given. (RD) May 8, 1849, (CLK) Wm. O. Young.

465) Third and final settlement of Mary Ann Winn, adm. of the estate of Thomas M. Winn, dec. May term, 1849.

Monies Expended: Wm. O. Young; Jno. Mosely; C. Stowers; R. B. Bronaugh; Estate of Stephen Cleaver; Estate of Valentine R. Matson; Isham O. Winn, as agent for Jemina Winn; Lawrence Taliasferro; John Ralls; E. W. Southworth; Thomas L. Anderson; Asbury Bramlet; Alexander Drummonds; Samuel Smith; W. O. Young; Mention of the Widow's children. (RD) May 8, 1849, (CLK) Wm. O. Young.

466) Seventh annual settlement of Elizabeth Weaver, adm. of the estate of Tilman Weaver, dec. May term, 1849.

Monies Expended: William Priest. (RD) May 8, 1849, (CLK) Wm. O. Young.

467) First annual settlement of Chapel Carstarphen, adm. of the estate of Thomas Williams, dec. May term, 1849.

Monies Expended: In 1849 to J. S. Buchanan; In 1845 to R. P. Strother for coffin; In 1846 to S. G. Ewing; In 1846 to Thos. Taylor; In January, 1849 to Jno. Ralls and Wm. O. Young. (RD) May 9, 1849, (CLK) Wm. O. Young.

468) Second annual settlement of James T. Hagar, adm. of the estate of Cornelius Lynch, dec. May term, 1849.

Monies Expended: Paid S. M. Rosser; On June 1, 1848 to S. K. Caldwell; On April 8, 1849 to Levi N. Boulware; On July 5, 1848 to Wm. O. Young; On July 18, 1848 to Mary R. Lynch; On December 5, 1848 to R. B. Caldwell; On January 1, 1849 to Hays & son; On May 17, 1847 for a note on W. H. Boulware charged on inventory to --- Lynch, dec. by James O. Hawkins; On May 17, 1847 for a note on John and John (sic) Stock; On May 17, 1849 for insolvent note on J. S. Ely; On October, 1848 for expenses to Wisconsin for estate on land; On June 4, 1849 to E. W. Southworth; On June 4, 1849 on insolvent note on James Boss, jr.; On January 1, 1849 to P. Coats, husband of Mary Coats; On January 1, 1849 to Mrs. Winnedred Briscoe; On January 1, 1849 to Sally C. Lynch; On January 1, 1849 to Jno. H. Lynch; On January 1, 1849 to J. B. Gore, guardian of W. B. Gore, heir of the deceased, by E. O. Lynch per power of attorney; On May 12, 1849 to Susan Leake to her agent, Barney M. Lynch; On May 12, 1849 to Wm. T. Gentry; Paid B. M. Lynch; paid J. Hagar. (RD) ?, (CLK) ?

469) Final settlement of Joshua Gentry, adm. of the estate of Rodes Gentry, dec. June term, 1849.

Monies Expended: --- Buchanan; John S. Turner. (RD) June 4, 1849, (CLK) William O. Young.

470) Second annual settlement of Drury Eads, adm. of the estate of John Dooley, dec. May term, 1849.

Monies Expended: Thomas Dooley, On November 25, 1844 to

Joseph Biggers; On November 27, 1844 to John Brownell; On December 2, 1844 to G. C. Hays for Mrs. Dooley, widow of Thomas Dooley; On December 3, 1844 to John Dooley; On January 1, 1845 to Wm. S. McClune; On January 1, 1845 to Matila Dooley; On April 12, 1845 to M. Dooley; On March 27, 1845 to J. S. Buchanan; On April 12, 1845 to J. Coleman; On April 26, 1845 to James Huls; On May 1, 1845 to M. Dooley; On May 7, 1845 to J. M. Crosthwait; On May 27, 1845 to Isaac Liter; On July 5, 1845 to M. Dooley; On July 4, 1845 to M. Dooley; On July 24, 1845 to M. Dooley; On March 23, 1846 to Isaac Scarce; On April 9, 1846 to J. S. Ely; On March 15, 1846 to O. Dooley; On September 17, 1846 to M. Dooley; On October 5, 1846 to M. Dooley; On May 18, 1847 to M. Dooley; On October 21, 1846 to John Ralls; On February 10,1848 to Wm. O. Young; On March 10, 1848 to J. S. Buchanan; On November 9, 1844 to M. Clayton; Paid Peter Smelser. (RD) June 4, 1849, (CLK) Wm. O. Young.

471) Second annual settlement of John D. Smith and Bartlet G. White, exrs. of the last will and testament of Stephen McPherson, dec. June term, 1849.

Monies Received: W. Mattox; ---Frasure; William Allen; ---Holt; Mrs. Keith; William Mattox; Isaah Marks; George Marks; John Marks; Keron H. Buchannon.

Monies Expended: Wm. Rush; --- Menefee; Mrs. Keith; James Glascock; Alexander McKuntry; --- Hardin; --- Glover; J. Dryden; J. Smith; Daniel Cohin; S. W. Watkins. (RD) June 2, 1849, (CLK) Wm. O. Young.

472) Second annual settlement of Joel Finks, adm. of the estate of Thomas Chedister, dec. July term, 1849.

Monies Expended: On March 20, 1849 to John F. Hawkins; On November 21, 1846 to J. J. Lyles; On November 2, 1846 to J. S. Strode. (RD) July 2, 1849, (CLK) William O. Young.

473) First annual settlement of James M. Bradley, adm. of the estate of Layton C. Bradley, dec. August term, 1849.

Monies Received: James M. Moss; Lyn B. Weakley; Nicholas N. Bradley.

Monies Expended: On August 26, 1848 to John Smith; On August 26, 1848 to H. Yager. (RD) August 6, 1849, (CLK) Wm. O. Young.

474) Fourth annual settlement of Charles Rice, surviving executor of the estate of Thomas Hicklin, dec. August term, 1849.

Monies Expended: On May 25, 1848 to William Boyd; On February 8, 1849 to Peter Smelser; On February 6, 1848 to J.V. Porter; On May 19, 1849 to Eliza Ann Tapley; On August 6, 1849 to Luke W. Watkins. (RD) August 6, 1849, (CLK) William O. Young.

475) Second settlement of William R. Campbell, adm. of the estate of William I. McElroy, dec. August term, 1849.

72

Monies Received: Sale of land on March 5, 1849; Cash from S. D. Biggs.
Monies Expended: On August 30, 1848 to W. T. Dubois; On September 1, 1848 to James Underwood and Alvin Menifee; On November 20, 1848 to C. J. McElroy; On January 1, 1849 to Wm. Young; On March 8, 1849 to Wm. J. McElroy; On March 8, 1849 to Allen Gallaher as guardian for the infant heirs; On March 12, 1849 to Saml. Muldrow; On March 26, 1849 to Wm. J. McElroy. (RD) August 7, 1849, (CLK) Wm. O. Young.

476) Third and final settlement of Jeremiah B. Vardeman and William H. Vardeman, exrs. of the estate of Jeremiah Vardeman, dec. August term, 1849.
Monies Expended: J. S. Buchanan; E. W. Southworth; William O. Young. (RD) August 7, 1849, (CLK) William O.Young.

477) Second annual settlement of Allen Rouse, adm. of the estate of Jonathan Hill, dec. September term, 1849.
Monies Expended: On September 11, 1848 to Widow Sarah Hill; On September 11, 1848 to J. J. Lyle; On March 11, 1848 to J. J. Lyle; On September 21, 1848 to Buchanan & Easton; On November 6, 1848 to O. Young; On June 24, 1849 to J. J. Lyle, Martin J. Lyle and Samuel Rouse; On June 24, 1849 to J. J. Lyle, John Millon, and Henry Snider; On July 18, 1849 to J. S. Buchanan; On March 26, 1849 to W. O. Young. (RD) September 3, 1839, (CLK) William O. Young.

478) Second annual settlement of Robert Hagar, adm. of Butler W. Brown, dec. August adjourned term, 1849.
Monies Expended: On September 1, 1848 to Charles Asher; On December 27, 1849 to Robert Bell; On September 2, 1848 to B. A. Spalding adm. of Thomas Brown; On August 15, 1848 to S K. Caldwell; On September 27, 1849 to Lucy Vardeman; On September 27, 1849 to Jer. Vardeman; On September 3 1849 to Henry McAtee. (RD) September 3, 1849, (CLK) William O Young.

479) First annual settlement of Ben A. Spalding, adm. of the estate of Ann S. Anderson, dec. August term 1849.
Monies Expended: On July 25, 1849 to George S. Hardy; On September 3, 1849 to J. A. Spalding; Paid Lewis S. Anderson; On August 29, 1849 to E C. Redman; On September 1, 1849 to Robert M. Spalding. (RD) September 3, 1849, (CLK) William O. Young.

480) Settlement of Thomas Clark, adm. of the estate of Charles Fuqua, dec. August adjourned term, 1849.
Monies Expended: Drs. Clayton & Strode; Mildred Ann Fuqua; William Tracy, Leonard Turley. (RD) September 3, 1849, (CLK) William Young.

481) First annual settlement of William Silver, adm. of the estate of James Daulton, dec. September term 1849.
Monies Expended: On September 9 1848 to Jacob Coffman; On October 9, 1848 to Wm. O. Young; On September 14, 1848 to J. P. Ament; On December 30, 1848 to John Daulton; On Sep-

tember 3, 1849 to McKenna & Settle. (RD) September 3, 1849, (CLK) William O. Young.

482) Second annual settlement of Hanceford Brown, adm. of Daniel Brown, dec. September term, 1849.

Monies Expended: J. D. S. Dryden, Richard Boyce, Charles Scandland, J. Doolin, Geo. W. Pattee, H. Brown. (RD) September 4, 1849, (CLK) Wm. O. Young.

483) Final settlement of Elizabeth Glascock, adm. of the estate of John Glascock, dec. August adjourned term, 1849.

Monies Expended: --- Buchanan, --- Jamison, H. Brown, S. W. Mayhall, Asa Glascock, G. F. Glascock, J. R. Floweree, C. Carstarphen, Green McFarland, --- Settle, Hamilton Hays, --- Jones.(RD) September 4, 1849, (CLK) Wm. O. Young.

484) First settlement of Samuel Smith, adm. of the estate of Robert Wright, dec. September term, 1849.

Monies Received: John Krigbaum, Wm. Ilor (?), Michael Gilbert, J. Shell, Saml. K. Caldwell, John G.B. Geery, John A. Wright, Archibald Organ, Thomas Mill.

Monies Expended: George C. Hays, Isham O. Winn, John Jamison, Wm. O. Young. (RD) September 5, 1849, (CLK) Wm. O. Young.

485) First annual settlement of Mary McGee, exr. of the estate of James McGee, dec. October term, 1849.

Monies Expended: B. S. Ely, William Ely. (RD) October 2, 1849, (CLK) ?

486) Fifth annual settlement of French Glascock, adm. of the estate of Charles Glascock, dec. November term, 1849.

Monies Received: On December 28, 1845 for the sale of the horse mill from T. H. Haden; In 1848 from J. S. Frazier; In 1848 from William Maddox; On March 3, 1846 from a note on John B. Paris, jr., and Daniel Wooden; On January 1, 1844 from J. Cochran; In 1844 for an account against Thomas Lmarr from January 1, 1845 for the lease of land.

Monies Expended: On February 4, 1849 for James C. Barnett's demand; On September 5, 1840 to Z. Merrett; On May 3, 1844 to M. I. Winn; On January --, 1845 to Spencer Glascock; On February 4, 1840 to Thomas Priest; On November 5, 1849 to John Ralls and Wm. O. Young. (RD) November 5, 1849, (CLK) Wm. O. Young.

487) First annual settlement of George S. Hardy, adm. of the estate of John N. Elsea, dec. November term, 1849.

Monies Received: On November 26, 1848 for the sale of the Boubuan claim; In 1848 from Joseph Kendrick.

Monies Expended: On October 27, 1848 to John W. Boulware; On November 28, 1848 to Isaac Ely; On November 10, 1848 to Wm. Jones; On November 1, 1848 to Elizabeth Elsea; On December 5, 1848 to Wm. H. H. Perry; On July 17, 1849 to J. P. Ament; In 1848 to W. Young; Paid for inventory by W.S. Elsea. (RD) November 9, 1849, (CLK) Wm. O. Young.

488) Second annual settlement of E. C. and L. H. Redman, adms. of the estate of Richard Redman, dec. November term, 1849.

Monies Expended: Richard N. Boyce; --- Spalding; William O. Young. (RD) November 5, 1850 (sic), (CLK) Wm. O. Young.

489) Second annual settlement of James Ely and Joshua Ely, adms. of the estate of Benjamin S. Ely, dec. November term, 1849.

Monies Expended: On December 5, 1848 to J. H. Keith; On November 3, 1849 to A. G. Galleher; On September 15, 1848 to Jo. Griffin; On November 5, 1848 to S. K. Caldwell; On February 5, 1849 to W. O. Young. (RD) November 5, 1849, (CLK) William O. Young.

490) Third annual settlement of Hanceford Brown, adm. of the estate of Robert M. McKay, dec. October term, 1849.

Monies Expended: John Glascock; David C. Skinner, Scarce, R. W. Lyons, Josiah Massie, Wm. G. Johnson, Walter M'Farland, James Smith, G. W. Fagan, James M. Creason, Walter Mace, John Jones, Thos. J. Ellis, William Cox. (RD) November 6, 1849, (CLK) Wm. O. Young.

491) First annual settlement of John T. Brizendine, adm. of the last will and testament of Lewis Brizendine, dec. November term, 1849.

Monies Received: In 1847 from Mr. Stewart.

Monies Expended: On July 9, 1845 to Wm. Tracy; On February 5, 1849 to Glascock and Tracy; On June 5, 1847 to David Payne and D. D. Dismukes; On September 15, 1845 to T.A. Purdom; On August 6, 1845 to Glascock and Tracy; On July 9, 1845 to Hays & Lampkin; On November 2, 1846 to R. W. Lyons; On March 24, 1847 to Isaac Scarce; On April 24, 1847 to D. P. and N. Fike; On January 5, 1847 to D. D. Dismukes; On October 6, 1845 to Walter Cartwill; On October 6, 1845 to J. J. K. Hawkins; On October 6, 1845 to T. R. Selms; On October 6, 1845 to C. A. Seamans for the hire of the slave, Sarah; Insolvent note as per court order dated November 3, 1845 on J. K. and Fanny Hawkins; On October 6, 1845 to John Garth for the hire of the slave, Albert; On November 3, 1845 per court order to Jacob and Juliann Saffel; On October 5, 1845 to Arnold & Richards; On October 5, 1845 to Daniel Brown; On October 6, 1845 to D.B. Young; On May 4, 1849 to J. Dudding; On May 4, 1849 to J. McCullough; Paid as a witness, E. W. Southworth; On May 4, 1849 paid Saml. Cross as exr. in case against --- Elgin. (RD) November 6, 1849, (CLK) William O. Young.

492) Final settlement of John D. Biggs, adm. of the estate of Robert Jamison, dec. August term, 1848. (sic)

Monies Received: On December 27, 1847 for the sale of the slave, Little Jim; Note on Robert Davis dated April 3, 1838.

Monies Expended: On December 27, 1847 to Robert Davis; On June 29, 1848 to Buchanan & Eastin; On September 1, 1847 to William Jamison; On November 7, 1849 to John Ralss; On June 1, 1846 to Wm. E. Harris; On June 1, 1846 to Isaac Searce. (RD) November 7, 1849, (CLK) Wm. O. Young.

493) First settlement of Jemima Tapley, exr. of the last will and testament of Joseph Tapley, dec. December term, 1849. (Note: Jemima Gillespie formerly Jemima C. Tapley.) No names given. (RD) December 3, 1849, (CLK) William O. Young.

494) First and final settlement of Martha A. V. Ewing, adm. of the will of Walker Carter, dec. December term, 1849. Monies Expended: Lucinda Carter, J. S. Buchanan, Wm. O. Young, Mrs. Carter. (RD) December 3, 1849, (CLK) ?.

495) Final settlement of Michael Jones, adm. of the estate of George Gillespie, dec. December term, 1849. Monies Expended: On September 5, 1846 to D. Jones; On November 5, 1849 to J. Ralls and --- Young; On August 8, 1848 to Saml. Smith; On November 6, 1848 to R. B. Caldwell; On September 4, 1848 to Cash & English; On November 27, 1848 to E. C. Murry; On November 6, 1848 to W. O. Young; On May 22, 1849 to Susan E. Gillespie; On November 5, 1849 to Susan E. Gillespie; On December 4, 1849 to E. W. Southworth. (RD) December 4, 1849, (CLK) William O. Young.

496) First annual settlement of Peter W. Pierce, adm. of the estate of Daniel Pollard, dec. December term, 1849. Monies Received: On November 6, 1848 from the sale of real estate. Monies Expended: On January 3, 1848 to J. S. Buchanan; On January 1, 1849 to William Tracy; On July 3, 1849 to Geo. C. Hays; On May 7, 1849 to Wm. O. Young; On January 22, 1849 to R. B. Caldwell; On December 4, 1849 E. H. Leake; On August 28, 1848 to S. T. Smith. (RD) December 3, 1839, (CLK) Wm. O. Young.

497) First annual settlement of Thomas Ely, dec., who died in the United States service by Ben A. Spalding, adm. December term, 1849. Monies Expended: Wm. Young. (RD) December 4, 1850 (?), (CLK) Wm. O.Young.

498) First annual settlement of Joseph J. Kendrick, adm. of the estate of William Mudd, dec. December term, 1849. Monies Received: On December 4, 1849 from the sale of the slave, John; On March 15, 1849 from --- Dubois. Monies Expended: On November 25, 1849 to John Blue; On September 3, 1849 to William Yancy; On December 15, 1848 to the Widow; On December 4, 1849 to Wm. O. Young; On December 4, 1849 to G.C. Hays; On November 29,1849 to Joshua Willson; On December 16, 1848 to Matthew Elliott; On January 1, 1848 to E. T. Bell. (RD) December 4, 1849, (CLK) Wm. O. Young.

499) Third and final settlement of William Priest, adm. of the estate of William S. Bast, dec. January term, 1850.

Monies Expended: John Ralls, Joseph Bower, Wm. Cleaver, Jacob Herlinger, Matthew McKenna, Peter C. Settles, William McFarland, Archibald Davis, Jackson Paris, Spencer Glascock, Abel Gregory, Lewis Garret, John Baynum, Joseph Dodd, French Glascock, Walter McFarland, J. S. Crosthwait, Marcus Hall, Laban White, --- McFarrin, Enoch Smis, Susan Galliher, Wm. O. Young. (RD) January 8, 1850, (CLK) William O. Young.

500) First annual settlement of Rosan Daniel, adm. of the estate of John N. Daniel, dec. January term, 1850.

Monies Expended: Dr. McElroy; Isaac Liters; J. S. Crosthwait. (RD) January 7, 1850, (CLK) ?

501) Settlement of Elizabeth Weaver, adm. of the estate of Tilman Weaver, dec. February term, 1850.

Monies Expended: William Priest. (RD) February 4, 1850, (CLK) William O. Young.

502) Second annual settlement of G. J. Thompson and Wm. P. Tapley, adm. of the estate of Hannah Tapley, dec. February term, 1850.

Monies Received: Note on James D. Dumkum.

Monies Expended: William Thompson, G. J. Thompson, Isaac D. Wilson, Reason Vermillion, Taylor Jones, Wm. Newland, J. M. Weatherford, Arthur Hern, John K. Hawkins, Widow Isabel, Jacob Herlinger, Caleb Ralls, George Cannon, T. A. Hayden, T. A. Haden (sic), James D. Dumkum, Cleaver & Thompson, R.B. Caldwell, J. C. Welborn. (RD) February 4, 1850, (CLK) Wm. O. Young.

503) First annual settlement of William Shick, adm. of the estate of Gabriel Snider, dec. February term, 1850.

Monies Expended: Wm. C. Phelps, Wm. O. Young. (RD) February 5, 1850, (CLK) William O. Young.

504) Final settlement of William Underwood and Sandie Hagan, adms. of the estate of Philip Myers, dec. January term, 1850.

Monies Expended: Joseph P. Ament, John Ralls, John A. Qualls, Wm. O. Henry, John Gatson, Jackson Crocket, Thomas C. Reid. (RD) February 5, 1850, (CLK) Wm. Young.

505) Second annual settlement of Fountain Kenney and William B. Norton, adms. of the estate of Thos. P. Norton, dec. February term, 1850.

Monies Received: Sale of house in Hannibal.

Monies Expended: On April 27, 1849 to Thomas Bell; On August 4, 1849 to George Scroter; On April 30, 1849 to James Elliott; On May 23, 1849 to George W. Barker; On May 23, 1849 to Wm. Allison; On November 27, 1849 to J.M. Elines; On June 2, 1849 to James Leake; On June 2, 1849 to John Byers; On June 2, 1849 to Benjamin Ely; On June 2, 1849 to Geo. L. Hardy; On August 6, 1849 to Samuel K. Caldwell; On August 6,

1849 to Matthew Elliott; On November 8, 1849 to John Blue; On November 18, 1849 to Joseph Heckett; On October 4, 1840 to Robert B. Caldwell; On December 8, 1849 to John Counts; On January 30, 1859 to George Whitecotton; On February 14, 1850 to John Ralls; On February 14, 1850 to Hanceford Brown. (RD) February 5, 1850, (CLK) William O. Young.

506) Final settlement of James Glascock, adm. of the estate of Lucy J. Glascock, sr., dec. February term, 1850.

Monies Received: Thomas M. Winn, Wm. McDaniel, Note on James Lampkin, Note on Jacinth Barnard, Note on Jefferson Glascock, Account on Petty & Fisher.

Monies Expended: On November 3, 1845 to Wm. H. Peake; On November 3, 1845 to Mrs. Cottle for midwifery; On April 1, 1849 for three sets of tombstones; On February 1, 1850 to --- Buchanan. (RD) February 5, 1850, (CLK) Wm. O. Young.

507) Final settlement of Jonathan Abbay, exr. of the estate of Jonathan Abbay, sr., dec. February term, 1850.

Monies Received: John R. Hall; Wm. C. and J. A. Abbay; Sale of slave, Jacob.

Monies Expended: Anthony Abbay, Levi F. Hall, William T. Dubois, R. & A. Abbay, Wm. O. Young, John Ralls, Thomas M. Campbell, James Underwood, J. Barnard, Luke W. Watkins, R.B. Caldwell, I. South, S. K. Caldwell. (RD) February 5, 1850, (CLK) Wm. O. Young.

508) First annual settlement of James Culbertson, adm. of Frances Purdom, dec. February term, 1850.

Monies Received: Note on H. W. Millman due December 20, 1847; Note on S. N. Brashears and Allen Brown due January 23, 1849; Rent of house from S. Caldwell due January 24, 1849; Note on Fanny Hawkins due January 22, 1849; Note on Jesse Hildreth; Note on Grason Dooley; Note on E. B. Strode; Note on Wm. O. Young; Note on Samuel K. Caldwell and Robert B. Caldwell due January 22, 1849; E. W. Southworth's receipt; William Tracy; A. C. Hawkins.

Monies Expended: Jesse Hildreth. Grason Dooley, William O. Young, S. K. Caldwell, Buchanan & Eastin, Taylor Jones, M. B. Jefferies, Mary King, C. F. Clayton, H. W. Wellman, Jesse Scarce, james W. Gallaher, Samuel Smith. (RD) February 6, 1850, (CLK) William O. Young.

509) Third and final settlement of John A. Wright and Corbin Benn, exr. of the estate of Joseph Wright, dec. August term, 1846. (sic)

Insolvent notes: Jesse Hildreth, T. A. Purdom, Posey N. Smith.

Monies Received: James C. Fox, William Krigbaum, Wm. Sisk, J. D. Biggs.

Monies Expended: On June 25, 1846 to J. S. Buchanan; On June 25, 1846 to N. T. Pierce; On December 3, 1842 to W. O. Young; On July 1, 1844 to John D. Biggs, On April 6, 1846 to

John D. Biggs, On January 1, 1845 to J. D. Biggs, On February 20, 1845 to --- Jones, adm. of --- Layne; On January 10, 1846 to --- Jones; On June 2, 1845 to --- Jones; On May 26, 1845 to --- Jones; On October 7, 1844 to --- Jones; On May 30, 1845 to J. D. Adkinson; On February 6, 1843 to R. Epperson; On February 3, 1845 to Patte, Elliott & Co.; On October 7, 1844 to Joseph D. Tapley; On April 9, 1845 to Joseph D. Tapley; On June 15, 1845 to Joseph D. Tapley; On January 1, 1846 to J. A. Wright, guardian for S. H. and Sanford Wright; On October 26, 1842 to James Hules; On Octboer 26, 1842 to J. A. Wright; On October 26, 1846 to W. C. Wright; On October 26, 1846 to C. Benn; On March 28, 1846 to W. C. Wright; On September 5, 1842 to C. Benn; On September 5, 1842 to S. B. Wright; On June 10, 1843 to William Briggs; Bankrupt Note on P. N. Smith; Bankrupt Note on F. G. Smith; Bankrupt Note on James Hulse; Note on Wm. Anderson; On August 6, 1846 to John Ralls.

Receipt Assignments: William Briggs; Corbin Benn; Wm. C. Wright; Saml. Reland, guardian; Saml. W. Mayhall; Peter W. Pierce.

Monies Expended: Scott B. Wright; William Briggs, who married Rhoda Wright, a child of the deceased; Corbin Benn, who married Elizabeth Wright, a child of the deceased; Saml. Reland, guardian of Polly Wright; Scott B. Wright of Bowling Green, Pike Co., Mo.; On February 7, 1850 to Wm. O. Youn. (RD) February 7, 1850, (CLK) William O.Young.

510) First annual settlement of James Culbertson, exr. of the estate of Peter Smelser, dec. April term, 1850.

Monies Received: On February 13, 1849 note on John A, Wright; Note on April 1, 1848 to --- Biggs; On April 1, 1848 to E. B. Strode and C. F. Clayton; On June 5, 1847 on Fowler & Weldy; Note on William Suttle and Thomas Buchanan; On January 2, 1847 to J. S. Crosthwait; On May 23, 1849 to H. H. Crooks; On October 14, 1848 to John J. Ely; On February 5, 1846 to R. B. and S. K. Caldwell; On February 5, 1846 to P. N. Norton; On November 22, 1848 on N. T. Pierce, --- Jones, --- Priest and --- Ralls; On May 2, 1848 to James Ely and D. and I. Griffith; On April 14, 1848 on Allen Sisk and R. B. Caldwell; On May 24, 1847 to J.S. Crosthwait and E. Allison; On February 17, 1845 to N. Fike and John Fike with the balance due May 24, 1848; On March 22, 1848 to Christian Liter; On October 24, 1848 to John A. Woods; On March 1, 1847 to A. H. Fike, A. Allison and J. G. Wylie; On March 27, 1848 to C. F. Clayton and P. Pierce; On March 27, 1848 to R. C. Briggs and George Waters.

Monies Expended: On March 27, 1849 to --- Jefferies; On May 2, 1849 to Henry Smelser, jr.; On June 4, 1849 to J. S. Buchanan; On July 2, 1849 to Isaac W. Ellis; On July 2, 1849 to G. C. Hays, jr.; On July 2, 1849 to William Tracy; On Au-

gust 28, 1849 to John Ralls; On August 27,1849 to G. Porter;
On April 22, 1849 to Mary A. Smelser, guardian; On January
10, 1850 to J. Briscoe, jr.; On February 15, 1850 to John
Liter; On February 25, 1850 to J. S. Buchanan; On March 1,
1850 to T. A. Taul; On March 4, 1850 to J. C. Welborn; On
March 13, 1850 to J. D. Biggs; On March 20, 1850 to N. Fike;
On March 27, 1850 H. H. Crooks; On February 13, 1850 to H.
Smelser, guardian; On February 13, 1850 to J. D. Biggs, guardian; On February 13, 1850 to Andrew J. Rice; On March 20,
1850 to H. Smelser, jr.; On March 23, 1850 to J. D. Biggs,
guardian; On April 1, 1850 to A. J. Rice; On April 1, 1850
to H. Smesler, guardian of Mary; On April 2, 1850 to McElroy
& Frazier; On April 2, 1850 John Ralls. (RD) April 2, 1850,
(CLK) Wm. O. Young.
   511) First annual settlement of Richard M. Brashears,
adm. of of the estate of John Tapley, dec., that was not
handled by the former administrator, Thomas Cleaver. May
term, 1850.
   Monies Received: Note on William Newland and William Maddox due December 3, 1849; Note on William Newland and Wil-
liam Maddox due on December 4, 1849; Note on John Boice due
April 19, 1847; Note on Jno. Ralls and N. T. Pierce due May
6. 1845; Note on McElroy & Sapeley due on March 23, 1847;
Note on Wm. O. Young and P. W. Pierce due On April 8, 1845;
Note on Pleasant Cox due November 1, 1841; Note on George
Glascock and J. Ralls due on April 19, 1847; Note on Charles
Glascock due on January 22, 1844; Note on Joseph Hardy and
S. Hepbron due on November 5, 1846; Note on Trammel Conn due
August 8, 1846; Note on G. C. Jeffries, R. Jeffries and A.
Fowler due on June 3, 1846; Note on R. B. Caldwell and J.
Jamison due on December 1, 1847; Note on Abner Smith due
Marach 23, 1847; Note on R. M. and Wm. Leake due on October
18, 1846; Note on J. R. Hagar and B. A. Spalding due on
March 24, 1847; Note on Allen Brown due on January 27, 1847;
Note on John Seely and Isaac Liter due on June 28, 1845;
Note on Abraham Liter due on September 17, 1845; Note on
James Kerr due on November 17, 1846; Note on R. M. Brashear
due on October 6, 1847; Note on J.J.T. McElroy and B.S. Ely
due on May 4, 1847; Note on Isaac Liter due on January 2,
1847; Note on Wm. Leake, Benj. Ely, Jas. Ely and Wm. Leake
due on July 7, 1847; Note on Walter M'Quie due on May 22,
1847; Note on Walter M'Quie due November 26, 1847; Note on
George Ledford due on September 25, 1843; Note on Elsey
Allison and J. S. Crosthwait due on January 23, 1847; Note
on Jas. J. T. McElroy due on January 20, 1847; Note on Matthew Smith due on January 9, 1844; Note on Eliza Caldwell
due om November 3, 1845; Note on Matthew Smith due on January 7, 1844; Note on William S. Tipton due on September 15,
1847; Note John and Benoni Bncei (?) due on April 19, 1847;

Note on Andrew Scott and Ab. Liter due on January 16, 1847; Geo. C. Frazier, J. J. T. McElroy and R. S. Reddish due on October 25, 1847; Note on Amos Ellis and John Chitwood due on September 22, 1846; Note on J. S. Crosthwait due on November 11, 1846; Note on John A. Woods due October 14, 1847; Note on John Ralls and J. T. Elzeas due on December 30, 1846; Note on Stephen and Geo. Glascock due on April 2, 1847; Note on Wm. C. Splawn and J. Ely due on August 23, 1844; Note on David Griffin and Jo. McGrew due February 8, 1847; Note on Geo. E. Frazier due October 27, 1847; Transcripts on Charles Rice dated March 5, 1844; Note on J. H. Humphreys due on January 23, 1847; Note on R. M. Leake and Wm. Leake due on January 2, 1849; Note on Eliza A. Tapley due on April 28, 1848; Note on R. M. Leake and J. S. Ledford due on April 28, 1848; Note on R. C. and J. C. Briggs due on April 28, 1848; Note on John D. Biggs due on April 28, 1848; Note on R. M. Brashears due on April 28, 1848; Note on G. W. Hendrick and T. Conn due on April 28, 1848; Note on Absalom Ellis and T. Conn due on April 28, 1848; Note on Wm. Boyd and Saml. M. Boyd due on April 28, 1848; Note on Wm. R. and John Coleman due on April 28, 1848; Note on Geo. Rice and W. O. Young due on April 28, 1848; Note on Chs. and Isaac Rice due on April 28, 1848; Note on C. Carstarphen due on April 28, 1848; Note on R. B. and S. K. Caldwell due on April 28, 1848; Note on William T. Briggs due on September 19, 1849; Note on Isaac Rice due on January 1, 1850; Note on Juden Norton due on April 28, 1848; Note on Thompson James due on July 10, 1849; Note on Thomas Cleaver due on April 2, 1849; Note on Jesse Rector due on May 26, 1849; Note on Robert Weldy due on April 28, 1848; Note on Eliza A. Tapley due on December 25, 1849; Note R. Boyer and Wm. Greathouse due on December 25, 1849; Note on J. Coleman and R. W. Hicklin due on December 25, 1849; Note on J. M. Leake and Wm. M. Leake due on December 25, 1849; Note on C. Rice and R. W. Hicklin due on December 25, 1849; Note on N. Fike and W. C. Splawn due on December 25, 1849; Note on Wm. Ardrey due on December 25, 1848; Note on Ashford Gore due on April 28, 1848; Note on John D. Bigg due on March 4, 1850; Note on John R. Scott and H. Allison due April 28, 1850.

Monies Expended: On May 19, 1849 to W. W. Powell; On June 8, 1849 to Saul & Ricketts; On June 8, 1849 to Eliza Tapley; On June 19, 1849 to McElroy & Frazier; On June 19, 1849 to Eliza Tapley; On May 3, 1850 to W. C. and B. B. Broughton; On January 1, 1850 to W. T. Davis; On September 24, 1849 to W. W. Powell.

Loss to the estate: On January 1, 1849 on the hire of the slave, Mariah, to Jas. M. Leake; On August 7, 1849 for the hire of the slave, Burr, to John Coleman. (RD) May 6, 1850, (CLK) William O. Young.

81

511) Second annual settlement of Hurt Yagar, adm. of the estate of Jason Berry, dec. May term, 1850.
Monies Expended: On May 6, 1849 to Wm. O. Young; On June 2, 1849 to G. S. Hardy; On May 6, 1850 to Matthew Elliott. (RD) May 6, 1850, (CLK) William O. Young.

512) Third annual settlement of John G, Sinklear, adm. of James Sneed, dec. May term, 1850.
Monies Expended: On February 5, 1850 to Chs. F. Clayton; On April 5, 1849 to T. Rodes; On March 13, 1850 to W. O. Young; R. B. Caldwell. (RD) May 6, 1850, (CLK) Wm. O. Young.

513) Third and final settlement of Fountain Kenney, adm. of the estate of John Kenney, dec.
Monies Expended: C. S. Taylor, W. O. Young, -- Buchanan. (RD) ?, (CLK) ?

514) Settlement of Samuel Smith, adm. of the estate of William H. H. Perry, dec. May term, 1850.
No names given. (RD) May 8, 1850, (CLK) William O. Young.

515) Final settlement of William Newland, exr. of the estate of Mary McClelland, dec. May term, 1850.
Monies Expended: On April 6, 1848 to Julia A. Miller; On January 15, 1849 to William Gerard, jr.; On October 15, 1848 to William Gerard, jr.; On March 5, 1850 to Joseph Hardy; On February 16, 1849 to R. B. Caldwell; John Ralls. (RD) May 7, 1850, (CLK) William O.Young.

516) Third annual settlement of Joel Finks, adm. of the Thomas R. Chedister, dec. May term, 1850.
Monies Expended: Paying of bond to Emily Ely (RD) June 3, 1850, (CLK) W. O. Young.

517) Third and final settlement of Robert Hagan adm. of Butler W. Brown, dec. June term, 1850.
Monies Expended: Raymond & Buchanan; Wm. O. Young; John Ralls. (RD) June 3, 1850, (CLK) Wm. O. Young.

518) Second and final settlement of B. A. Spalding, adm. of the estate of Thomas Brown, dec. June term, 1850.
Monies Received: On June 3, 1850 from Robt. Hagan, adm. of B. W. Brown, dec.
Monies Expended: Wm. O. Young, J. P. Ament, John Ralls. (RD) June 3, 1850, (CLK) W. O. Young.

519) First annual settlement of James Kerr, adm. of the estate of John Brownell, dec. June term, 1850.
Monies Expended: Brashear & Griffin, John Ralls. (RD) June 3, 1850, (CLK) Wm. O. Young.

520) Fourth annual settlement of Richard M. Brashear, adm. of the estate of Otho Brashear, dec. June term, 1850.
Monies Expended: Wm. O. Young, S. W. Watkins, W. F. Treadway. (RD June 4, 1850, (CLK) W. O. Young.

521) Final settlement of William Gerard, adm. of the estate of Alexander Gerard, dec. May term, 1850.
Monies Expended: John Ralls, --- Galleher W. O. Young.

Saml. Lyle. (RD) June 4, 1850, (CLK) William O. Young.
522) Third and final settlement of Benjamin A. Spalding,
adm. of the estate of John M. Kelsey, dec. May adjourned
term, 1850.
Monies Expended: William T. Bond, J. Biggs, Mention of
trip to Shelbyville. (RD) July 1, 1850, (CLK) William O.
Young.
523) Second and final settlement of Benjamin A. Spalding, adm. of the estate of Ann S. Anderson, dec. May adjo-
urned term, 1850.
Monies Expended: S. S. Anderson, J. H. Anderson, W. O.
Young, Joseph P. Ament. (RD) July 1, 1850, (CLK) William O.
Young.
524) Third and final settlement of Jas. T. Hagan, adm.
of the estate of Cornelius N. Lynch, dec. July term, 1850.
Monies Expended: M. Elliott, E.O. Lynch, R.B. Caldwell,
Lawson Berry's Estate, Ignatius J. Spalding, J. A. Spalding,
W. S. and J. W. Lampton, W. Leake, Raymond & Buchanan, R. S.
Reddish, Milton B. McElroy, Susan Leake, E. W. Southworth,
W. O. Young, (RD) July 2, 1850, (CLK) William Young.
525) First settlement of Allison R. Maddox, adm. of the
estate of Francis Conn, dec. August term, 1850.
Monies Received: --- Johnson, --- Stower, Levi Hatcher,
William Hardy, --- Severs.
Monies Expended: On October 25, 1849 to Nancy Conn; On
October 17, 1849 to J. P. Richards, On November 5, 1849 to
S. K. Caldwell, On January 5, 1850 to --- Lewellen, On Janu-
ary 8, 1850 to G. W. Sowers, On September 12, 1849 to J. M.
Mills, On December 29, 1849 to T. R. Selms, On December 3,
1849 to William O. Young, On February 20, 1850 to John B.
Truitt, On January 8, 1850 to Weldy, Ellis & Clark, On April
1, 1850 to Joseph C. McGrew, On December 31, 1849 to T. Conn
for the benefit of Francis Williams, On August 6, 1850 to H.
A. Harris, On August 6, 1850 to John Ralls, Wm. O. Young and
J. S. Buchanan. (RD) August 6, 1850, (CLK) William O. Young.
526) Second annual settlement of Joseph J. Kendrick,
adm. of the estate of William Mudd, dec. August term, 1850.
Monies Received: On January 28, 1850 from E. T. Bell, On
May 8, 1850 on Saml. Smith.
Monies Expended: On February 28, 1850 to J. T. Hagan,
adm. of C. N. Lynch; On February 23, 1850 to S. T. Elliott;
On December 4, 1849 to R. B. Caldwell; On April 13, 1850 to
James Mason; On December 15, 1849 to Benjamin Ely; On Decem-
ber 4, 1849 to J. S. Crosthwait; On December 1, 1848 to John
M. Calhoun for coffin and order accepted by Elizabeth Mudd;
On August 6, 1849 paid Geo. Whitecotton on account allowed
in J. J. T. McElroy vs. W. Mudd, dec.; On February 16, 1850
to Henry Thomas; On August 6, 1849 to George Whitecotton; On
January 28, 1850 to J. Blue; On January 8, 1850 to G. S.

83

Hardy, On December 28, 1849 to B. A. Spalding, On December 29, 1849 to W. S. Elsea, On August --, 1850 to E. W. Southworth. (RD) August 6, 1850, (CLK) Wm. O. Young.

527) Third and final settlement of William R. Campbell, adm. of the estate of William J. McElroy, dec. August term, 1850.

Monies Received: J. D. Biggs.

Monies Expended: R. B. Caldwell, Wm. O. Young, Raymond & Buchanan, A. Cooper, E. W. Southworth, A. G. Gallaher., Wm. R. Campbell. (RD) August 6, 1850, (CLK) Wm. O. Young.

528) First annual settlement of Benjamin A. Spalding, adm. of the estate of John Bell, dec. August term, 1850.

No names given. (RD) August 7, 1850, (CLK) Wm. O. Young.

529) Third and final settlement of Abraham Buford, adm. of the estate of John Buford, dec. August term, 1850.

Monies Expended: On May 3, 1841 to --- Slosson; On September 14, 1841 to A. & W. McMurty; On April 17, 1842 to T. D. Reed; On July 9, 1843 to G. C. Stamp; On August 5, 1850 to Smith & Son; On June 15, 1842 to --- McMurty; On March 22, 1841 to Wm. G. Johnson; On August 5, 1850 to Jas. Gerrish; On November 3, 1840 to W. R. Waller; On July 10, 1841 to J. Wright; On February 2, 1841 to Hays & Blair. (RD) August 7, 1850, (CLK) William Young.

530) First annual settlement by George D. Muldrow, adm. of the estate of Samuel Muldrow, dec. September term, 1850.

Monies Received: Estate of Wm. J. McElroy.

Monies Expended: R. B. Caldwell. (RD) September 3, 1850, (CLK) William O. Young.

531) Third annual settlement of Geo. G. Muldrow, adm. of the estate of Andrew Muldrow, dec. February term,1850 (sic)

Monies Received: Hire of slaves, Richard and Eliza, by C. Muldrow; Hire of slave, Alice, by J. Barnard, Hire by the administrator the slave, Robert, Negro sold to --- Vandeventer; Hire of the slave, Mary, by C. Muldrow.

Monies Expended: On March 1, 1847 to Walker Southan; On February 28, 1850 to Charlotte T. Muldrow; On December 5, 1849 to Foster Ray; On September 4, 1848 to Clement White; On March 5, 1850 to W. Southan; On June 5, 1849 to J. B. White; On August 14, 1849 to W. Southan; On September 4, 1848 to Clement White; On June 5, 1849 to S. T. Rhodes; On March 16, 1849 to B. Edelin, adm. of the McElroy estate; On August 1, 1849 to Allen G. Gallaher; On August 7, 1849 to S. W. Caldwell; On September 4, 1849 to J. Ralls; On January 2, 1849 to Wm. O. Young; On March 2, 1850 to Wm. Underwood; On November 30, 1849 to B. B. King; On March 5, 1850 to E. W. Southworth. (RD) September 2, 1850, (CLK) ?

532) Fifth annual settlement of Charles Rice, exr. of the estate of Thomas Hickton. October term, 1850.

No names given. (RD) October 7, 1850, (CLK) Wm. O. Young.

533) Final settlement of Thomas Clark, adm. of the estate of Charles C. Fuqua, dec. October term, 1850. Monies Received: Rent of land for 1850 due January 1, 1851.
Monies Expended: On October 1, 1844 for a note on Christain Straube who refuses to pay; Raymond & Buchanan; Wm. O. Young, John Ralls. (RD) October 8, 1850, (CLK) Wm. O. Young.

534) Third settlement of Allen Rouse, adm. of the estate of Jonathan Hill, dec. October term, 1850.
Monies Received: Mention of sale of real estate.
Monies Expended: On July 22, 1850 to Raymond & Buchanan; On November 23, 1849 to R.B. Caldwell; On February 12, 1848; On November 6, 1845 to Lovel Rouse; On March 11, 1848 to Levi N. Boulware; On November 13, 1847 to John Wills; On October --, 1847 to John S. Thompson; On October 5, 1850 to Samuel Smith; On October 5, 1850 to W. O. Young; On October 7, 1850 to E. W. Southworth; On October 7, 1850 to Rebecca A. Hill. (RD) October 8, 1850, (CLK) William O. Young.

535) Second annual settlement of Samuel Smith, adm. of the estate of Robert Wright, dec. October term, 1850.
Monies Received: John Krigbaum; William Inlow; Shell's note; J.B. Geary; Thos. Mills; Archibald Bryan; Jno. Wright. (RD) October 9, 1850, (CLK) William O. Young.

536) Final settlement of James Kerr, adm. of the estate of John Brownell, dec. November term, 1850.
Monies Expended: -- Croshwait; Wm. O. Young; John Ralls; J. P. Ament. (RD) November 4, 1850, (CLK) Wm. O. Young.

537) First annual settlement of Wilkinson Crawford, adm. of the estate of Jno. M. Crawford, dec. November term, 1850.
Monies Expended: Presley Darnes; Wilkinson & Herndon; S. K. Caldwell; John T. Wills; Allen Rouse; Widow's receipt from Hannah Crawford; Wm. O. Young. (RD) November 4, 1850, (CLK) William O. Young.

538) First annual settlement of William Stone, adm. of the estate of Susannah Riddle, dec. November term, 1850.
Monies Received: Mention of receiving money from Great Britain.
Monies Expended: Mrs. Stone, John N. Riddle's heirs, Wm. O. Young, On August 24, 1850 to James N. Riddle, On August 24, 1850 to William N. Riddle, On August 29, 1850 to David H. Riddle, On October 25, 1850 to Catherine B. Stone. (RD) November 6, 1850, (CLK) William O. Young.

539) Third annual settlement of John O. Smith and Bartlett G. White, exrs. of the estate of Stephen McPherson, dec. November term, 1850.
Monies Received: Note on Mr. Hughes; Note on Mr. League of Hannibal; Note on Jeptha P. Smith; Note on Geo. C. Light; Note on Mr. Hopkins.
Monies Expended: On June 5, 1849 to William O. Young; On

October 7, 1849 to Rackliff & Morton; On April 5, 1850 to R. B. Caldwell; On November 18, 1849 to W. S. Fletcher; On November 18, 1849 to Dr. Rhodes; On November 18, 1849 to W. Y. Morrow; On March 26, 1850 to E. Hopkins; On March 26, 1850 to Alex McMurty; On March 26, 1850 to Lakeman & Sutherland; On March 26, 1850 to Cleaver's demand; On March 26, 1850 to to Wm. O. Young. (RD) November 6, 1850, (CLK) William O. Young.

540) Final settlement of James G. Wylie, adm. of the estate of Pleasant Cox, dec. July term, 1846. (sic)

Monies Received: On May 3, 1845 from A. Briscoe; In October, 1843 for the rent of house in Hannibal by S. R. H. Wylie; In October, 1844 rent of house from --- Hays.

Monies Expended: Paid November 1, 1841 the following persons: S. Cleaver, John Ledford, John Fuqua, Free Jack, James Davis, Samuel C. Rubey, Wm. C. Wylie, Jos. F. Abington, Wm. C. Wright, J. E. Gatewood, George Eales, R. Snodgrass, Heath Jones, M. Cox, Peake & McKay, Samuel W. Cox, Charlotte Cox, J. Hawkins, J. S. Buchanan, George C. Hays, A. & W. McMurty; Paid on February 5, 1844 to Buchanan & Rice; On November 1, 1841 to John Tapley; On December 9, 1846 to Isaac Scarce; On December 6, 1842 to Emison & Shields; On February 9, 1842 to M'Kay & Peake; On July 7, 1842 to John Ralls; On February 9, 1842 to Wm. O. Young. (RD) November 6, 1850, (CLK) William O. Young.

541) First annual settlement of John M. Johnson, adm. of the estate of Joseph K. Johnson, dec. December term, 1850.

Monies Expended: On October 5, 1849 to J. Coffman; In 1849 to Rackliffe & Morton; On October 6, 1849 to F. Jett; On October 31, 1849 to to Glascock & Hawkins; On November 5, 1849 to Wm. O. Young; On November 5, 1849 to J. S. Buchanan; On January 8, 1850 to R. B. Caldwell; In 1849 to R. B. Caldwell; On February 15, 1850 to W. O. Young; On October 31, 1850 to Mellon & Hawkins; On November 1, 1849 to W.H. Cohen; On November 1, 1849 to N. P. Runkle; In 1850 to R. J. Rudisill; On December 2, 1850 to Wm. O. Young. (RD) December 2, 1850, (CLK) William O. Young.

542) First annual settlement of Martha A. V. Ewing, adm. of the estate of Samuel G. Ewing, dec. December term, 1850.

Monies Expended: Nancy Cottle, Geo. Smith, --- Jamison, Wm. O. Young. (RD) December 2, 1850, (CLK) Wm. O. Young.

543) Second annual settlement of George S. Hardy, adm. of the estate of John N. Elsea, dec. November term, 1850.

Monies Received: Estate of Wm. H. H. Perry, Mrs. See.

Monies Expended: On January 12, 1850 to the Widow; On February 3, 1848 to --- Caldwell; On February 10, 1849 to --- Caldwell; On November 21, 1850 to --- Caldwell; On January 2, 1850 to S. S. Anderson; On September 25, 1849 to E. Peck; On November 17, 1849 to the Widow; On March 21, 1850 to H. B. Dillard; On May 7, 1850 to Benjamin Ely; On May 31, 1850 to the Widow; On July 22, 1850 to James Leake; On October 21, 1850 to William Elzea; On October 5, 1850 to Robert T. Able; On August 31, 1850 to David Blue; On November 4, 1850 to S. S. Caldwell; In March, 1850, to S. H. Gardner; On November 16, 1850 to T. Hardesty;On November 13, 1850 to Wm. Greathouse; On November 13, 1850 to A. G. Gallaher; On November 15, 1850 to the Widow; On November 29, 1850 to the following: E. C. Redmon, Jacob Morgan, A. Green, J.O. Smith, John M. Thompson, Bernard Lewellen; On December 2, 1850 to George Whitecotton; On December 2,1850 to Wm. O. Young. (RD) December 4, 1850, (CLK) Wm. O. Young.

544) Final settlement of Gilbert J. Thompson and William P. Tapley, adms. of the estate of Hannah Tapley, dec. February term, 1851.

Monies Received: Dabney Jones, Jonathan Bird, Wm. P. Tapley, G. I. Thompson.

Monies Expended: On February 5, 1850 to John Ralls; On March 4, 1850 to John D. Biggs; On March 13, 1840 to Adam Mase; On May 6, 1850 to Anderson Briscoe; On May 6, 1850 to John Mase; On May 6, 1850 to William Jones; On June 12, 1850 to William Jones, for T. Cleaver; Saml. Smith; A. Briscoe, for T. Cleaver; A. Brown; Clemens; D. Jones; Turner Haden; P. Lyons. (RD) February 3, 1851, (CLK) Wm. O. Young.

545) Third annual settlement of Thomas Cleaver, exr. of the estate of S. Cleaver, dec. February term, 1851.

Monies Received: On August 1, 1848 from R. B. Caldwell; On September 7, 1848 from G. I. Thompson; On August 1, 1848 from Henry Early; On August 1, 1848 to William English; On August 1, 1848 From Heath Jones; On August 1, 1848 from W.B. Rogers; On August 1, 1848 from French Glascock; On December 1, 1848 from William Newland; On December 1, 1848 from Peter Pierce; On February 7, 1849 from Isaac Wilson; On February 14, 1849 from John Ralls; On March 28, 1849 from J. Wilson; On March 28, 1849 from Thomas Winn; On March 28, 1849 from Peter Pierce; On April 4, 1849 from Jas. Dunkum; On April 4, 1849 from A. Briscoe; On April 4, 1849 from James Dimmitt; On April 4, 1849 from the estate of John Glascock; On April 4, 1849 from Luke W. Watkins; On April 4, 1849 from John Ralls; On April 4, 1849 from John Ralls; On April 4, 1849 from Reason Vermillion; On April 3, 1849 from William Newland; On April 3, 1849 from the estate of Hannah Tapley; On April 3, 1849 from McPherson's estate; On April 3, 1849 from Nelson Fike; On April 3, 1849 from Gerry Butler; On April 3, 1849 from Thornton Binzendine; On April 3, 1849 from A. Briscoe; On April 3,1849 from Cross & Newland; On April 3, 1849 from W. O. Young; On April 3, 1849 from William Gerrard; On April 3, 1849 from Hosea Northcut; On April 3, 1849 from Gerrard & Martin; On April 3, 1849 from Grayson Doolin; On

March 26, 1850 from A.C. Hawkins; On March 1, 1850 from Hanceford Brown; On March 1, 1846 from Stephen Glascock; On October 1, 1845 from William Caldwell; On March 1, 1846 from John Ralls; On March 1, 1846 from Thos. Cleaver; On September 9, 1849 from Granville Clayton; On February 18, 1846 from Joel Ledford; On February 18, 1846 from Saml. O. Cross; On November 6, 1842 from David Glascock; On November 6, 1842 from John K. Hawkins.

Monies Expended: On April 2, 1849 to the following: may Cleaver, William Jones, John A. Cobbs, Anderson Briscoe, Wm. Cleaver, Henry Cleaver, Joel Ledford, E. W. Southworth, W. O. Young, D. D. Dismukes, R. B. Caldwell, Luke W. Watkins, William Fuqua, Saml. K. Caldwell, Robert Lyons, A. J. Harrison, Robert Sinkclear, A. Briscoe. (RD) February 4, 1851, (CLK) Wm. O. Young.

546) Third and final settlement of E.C. Redman and L. H. Redman, by Elias Redman, acting administrator, of the estate of Richard Redman, dec. February term, 1851.

Monies Expended: E. W. Southworth, J. Scarce, S.K. Caldwell, Wm. O. Young, --- Clemens, John Jamison. (RD) February 4, 1851, (CLK) Wm. O. Young.

547) First annual settlement of Ulysses Norton, adm. of the estate of Richard Norton, dec. February term, 1851.

Monies Received: T. I. Ellis, Jas. J. T. McElroy.

Monies Expended: On February 9, 1850 to Raymond & Buchanan; On August 27, 1850 to Dr. F. Jett; On October 7, 1850 to John M. Graves; On December 16, 1850 to Martin Leister; On December 11, 1850 to G. S. Hardy; On December 4, 1850 to D. Smith. (RD) February 4, 1851, (CLK) Wm. O. Young.

548) Second annual settlement of Samuel Smith, adm. of the estate of William H. H. Perry, dec. February term, 1851.

Monies Received: Rent of farm in 1850; Wm. S. Tipton; Robt. Leake.

Monies Expended: S. Reed; A. Mudd, Trammel Conn. (RD) February 6, 1851, (CLK) Wm. O. Young.

549) Final settlement of Hanceford Brown, adm. of the estate of Daniel Brown, dec. August term, 1849. (sic)

Monies Expended: John Govny, S. K. Caldwell, T. A. Purdom, James Culbertson, Abraham and Alexander Buford, Joseph Rice, Wm. O. Young, Jos. Rice (guardian), Allen Brown (guardian), William I. Brown (guardian), John Ralls, Clayton & Strode, --- Southworth. (RD) February 6, 1851, (CLK) Wm. O. Young.

550) First annual settlement of Norman Robinson, adm. of the estate of Benjamin Robinson, jr., dec. March term, 1851.

Monies Expended: On October 3, 1850 to Henry Couch; On February 3, 1851 to Dr. T. Rodes; On June 4, 1850 to Raymond & Buchanan; On June 4, 1850 to Eliz. Robinson. (RD) March 3, 1851, (CLK) Wm. O. Young.

551) First annual settlement of Ben A. Spalding, adm. of

the estate of William Lambeth, dec. March term, 1851.
Monies Received: Cash received from E. W. Southworth, attorney, from the War Department.
Monies Expended: On June 4, 1850 to Wm. O. Young, On March 5, 1850 to C. Carstarphen. (RD) March 4, 1851, (CLK) Wm. O. Young.

552) Third and final settlement of James Ely and Joshua Ely, adms. of the estate of Benjamin S. Ely, dec. April term, 1851.
Monies Received: Rent of land in Audrain County for 1849, Jacob Welty.
Monies Expended: William S. Ely, as an heir; Myers & McElroy; On April 7, 1851 to E. W. Southworth; On August 6, 1849 to --- M'Elroy; On August 6, 1851 to H. B. Fagan; On August 6, 1849 to Stephen Scobee; On February 21, 1851 to Jacob Welty; On November 6, 1850 to O. Clemens; On January 28, 1851 to Jno. H. Keith; In December, 1849 to John Ralls and Wm. O. Young. (RD) April 8, 1851, (CLK) Wm. O. Young.

553) Second annual settlement of James Culbertson, adm. of the estate of Frances Purdom, dec. April term, 1851.
Monies Expended: On April 7, 1851 to Allen Brown; On March 1, 1851 to Clayton & Strode; On March 4, 1851 to Peter W. Pierce; On March 25, 1851 to Wm. O. Young; On January 13, 1851 to G. C. Hays; On January 13, 1851 to Spencer Glascock; On February 3, 1851 to R. P. Kelley. (RD) April 8, 1851, (CLK) Wm. O. Young.

554) Second annual settlement of James Culbertson, adm. of the estate of Peter Smelser, dec. April term, 1851.
Monies Expended: On May 21, 1850 to W. O. Young; On June 3, 1850 to Clayton & Strode; On January 11, 1851 to Henry Smelser, jr.; On April 7, 1851 to Henry Smelser, jr.; On April 7, 1851 to A.J. Rice; On April 7, 1851 to Joseph Smelser, guardian; On April 7, 1851 to Mary A. Kelly. (RD) April 7, 1851, (CLK) Wm. O. Young.

555) First annual settlement of Allen G. Gallaher, adm. of the estate of James T.T. McElroy, dec. April term, 1851.
Monies Received: N. G. Leake, trustee of Raphael Leake; Isaac Liters.
Monies Expended: On March 25, 1850 to Raymond & Buchanan; On February 6, 1850 to Jas. A. Irvine; On March 7, 1850 to John K. Hawkins; On March 8, 1850 to Margaret A. McElroy; On May 6, 1850 to J. M. Mills; On June 5, 1850 to Jordan and Buford; On May 9, 1850 to P. A. Salling; On May 9, 1850 to T. M. Campbell; On May 9, 1850 to Joshua Ely; On May 9, 1850 to H. G. Martin; On December 20, 1850 to Shute & Davis; On December 3, 1850 to A. McElroy; On December 3, 1850 Jerry Wade; On December 24, 1850 to William O. Young; On March 15, 1851 to --- Brashear, adm. of the estate of John Tapley; On March 22, 1851 to R. Nelson; In 1850 to Mrs. Sheckles; On

March 14, 1850 to J. M. Calhoun.

Accounts Charged On Inventory: John Salling, Saml. Muldrow, Samuel Rouse, Lewis S. Anderson, Robert Arron, Joseph Hardy, Joseph N. Barr, George Whitecotton, Frank Leake, H. Boulware, John M. Leake, Widow Leake, Henry Gardner. (RD) April 9, 1851, (CLK) William O. Young.

556)   First annual settlement of George E. Frazier, surviving partner of James T. T. McElroy, dec. April term, 1851.

No names given. Accounting of the gross receipts and expenditures of the firm for 1847, 1848, 1849, 1850. (RD) April 9, 1847, (CLK) William O. Young.

557) First settlement of Nancy Conn, adm. of the will of of Francis Conn, dec. August term, 1851.

Monies Received: John D. Biggs, James Cox, William D. Coxe (sic), Andrew J. Rice, David L. Maddox, G. W. Somers, George Glascock, Robert C. Briggs. (RD) August 5, 1851, (CLK) W. O. Young.

558)   First annual settlement of James Ely, adm. of the estate of William P. Ely, dec. April term, 1852. (sic)

Monies Received: Rent of farm for 1851; Rent of wheat land for 1851; Money from J. S. Ely.

Monies Expended: James Underwood, J. R. Biggers, H. G. Martin, A. G. Gallaher, Wm. O. Young, O. Clemens, James Ely. (RD) April 6, 1852 (sic), (CLK) William O. Young.

559) Final settlement of Joel Finks, adm. of the estate of Thomas R. Chedester, dec. May term, 1851.

Monies Expended: W. O. Young. (RD) May 5, 1851, (CLK) W. O. Young.

560) Final settlement of Hiram W. Glascock, adm. of the estate of Eliza Rhodes, dec. May term, 1851.

Monies Expended: R.B. Caldwell, John Ralls, C. B. Clark, Joseph P. Ament, Nelson Fike, Carty Wells, D. P. Fikes, W. H. Peak, Eliza Glascock, Leroy Glascock, Asa Glascock, Leroy Glascock (guardian of William H. Glascock, James H. Glascock and Martha J.Glascock), E. W. Southworth, James Culbertson, Estate of Asa Glascock, dec., Allen Brown, William O. Young, John Jamerson. (RD) May 6, 1851, (CLK) William O. Young.

561) First annual settlement of James M. Mills and Charles W. Mills, adms. of the estate of James Mills, sr., dec. August term, 1851.

Monies Expended: On August 2, 1851 to William Priest; On July 31, 1851 to Y. O. Selmer; In 1850 to W. Crawford; On June 1,,1850 to B. Y. Norlen; On November 18, 1850 to R. F. Richmond; On December 7, 1850 to Saml. Smith; On December 7, 1850 to Y.R. Selmer; On December 7, 1851 to Joseph P. Ament; On December 7, 1851 to Harrison & Hawkins; On November 2, 1850 to Y. R. Selmer; On November 11, 1850 to J. W. Mills; On November 11, 1850 to Henry A. Harris; On November 11,

1850 to J.W. Mills; On November 11, 1850 to E.W. Southworth.
(RD) August 6, 1851, (CLK) William O. Young.

562) Final settlement of Branch Hatcher, adm. of the estate of Stephen P. Cook, dec. September term, 1851.
Monies Expended: Mention of boarding and clothing of heirs, but no names are stated. (RD) September 1,1851, (CLK) W. O. Young.

563) First annual settlement of William Shuck, adm. of the estate of Henry Snider, dec. September term, 1851.
Monies Expended: Raymond & Buchanan, W. O. Young. (RD) September 2, 1851, (CLK) W. O. Young.

564) Second annual settlement of George G. Muldrow, adm. of the estate of Samuel Muldrow, dec. September term, 1851.
Monies Received: W. J. McElroy, W. Bigger.
Monies Expended: J. J. T. McElroy; On December 27, 1850 to S. Smith; On February 3, 1851 to -- Buchanan; Joshua Ely; W. Young; A. G. Galleher. (RD) September 2, 1851, (CLK) W. O. Young.

565) Fifth and final settlement of Samuel B. Caldwell and Elizabeth Robinson, adms. of the estate of Benjamin Robinson, dec. September term, 1851.
Monies Expended: John Ralls, W. O. Young, Mrs. E. Robinson, S. B. Caldwell. (RD) September 2, 1851, (CLK) W. O. Young.

566) Sixth annual settlement of French Glascock, adm. of the estate of Charles Glascock, dec. August adjourned term, 1851.
Monies Received: Thos. Bowling, Arh. Hawkins.
Monies Expended: Richard M. Brashear, adm. of J. Tapley. (RD) October 7, 1851, (CLK) W. O. Young.

567) First annual settlement of Ben A. Spalding, adm. of the estate of James Andrews, dec. November term, 1851.
Monies Expended: -- Hagar, -- Elzea, -- Majin, -- Wooten. (RD) November 4, 1851, (CLK) W. O. Young.

568) First annual settlement of W. H. Smith, adm. of the estate of John Harbinger, dec. November term, 1851.
Monies Received: Sale Bill dated November 2, 1850.
Monies Expended: J. P. Ament, the Widow. (RD) November 4, 1851, (CLK) W. O. Young.

569) Second annual settlement of William Stone, adm. of the estate of Susannah Riddle, dec. November term, 1851.
Monies Expended: Mention of the heirs of John N. Riddle, dec.; On July 4, 1850 to Raymond & Buchanan; On April 4, 1851 to Capehart & Bradford; On April 4, 1851 to W.B. Quinn; On October 10, 1851 to the West Ely Presbyterian Church per order of W. N., Jas. W., D. H. Riddle and Catherine Stone; On October 10, 1851 to Susan Riddle for the heirs of John N. Riddle, dec.; On November 1, 1851 to Susan Riddle, mother of the heirs of John N. Riddle, dec. (RD) November 4, 1851,

(CLK) W. O. Young.

570) Fourth and final settlement of Joseph J. Kendrick, adm. of the estate of William Mudd, dec. November term, 1851.

Monies Received: On December 25, 1849 for the hire of the slaves, John and Charles.

Monies Expended: W. O. Young, J. P. Ament, E. W. Southworth. (RD) November 4, 1851, (CLK) W. O. Young.

571) First annual settlement of John Chitwood, adm. of the estate and will of Seth Chitwood, dec. November term, 1851.

Monies Received: Cash from A. Smith for the hire of the slave, Sam; Cash from Stephen Burch on the division of the slave, Sam, alias Samuel; Slave, Jack, partitioned to John Chitwood; Slave, Delila and child, partitioned to H. Chitwood; Slave, Fanny, kept by Y. Chitwood; Slave, Littleton, partitioned to Amos Chitwood per agreement filed in the county court on July 8, 1850; Notes on inventory to W. S. Lofland, N. T. Pearce and Wm. Carson; Mention of the sale of land.

Monies Expended: Slave, Littleton, distributed to Amos Chitwood; Slaves, Delila and child, distributed to Hiram Chitwood; Slave, Sam, distributed to Stephen Burch; James Chitwood; Richard Chitwood; Slave, Jack, distributed to John Chitwood. (RD) November 5, 1851, (CLK) W. O. Young.

572) First annual settlement of James A. Emison, adm. of the estate of James Turley, dec. November term, 1851.

Monies Received: Sale Bill filed November 15, 1850.

Monies Expended: R. Watson, A. McGinnis, John Strain, Menefee & Mills, Lampton & Hays, Henry Bigler, On July 9, 1851 to Oney Carstarphen, On December 26, 1850 to S. Smith, On October 31, 1851 to G. W. Johnson, S. K. Caldwell, and W. O. Young. (RD) November 5, 1851, (CLK) W. O. Young.

573) Second annual settlement of Wilkinson Crawford, adm. of the estate of John M. Crawford, dec. January term, 1852.

Monies Expended: William Crawford, Thomas Bell, Saml. Smith. (RD) January 5, 1852, (CLK) W. O. Young.

574) Second annual settlement of John M. Johnson, adm. of the estate of Joseph K. Johnson, dec.

No names given. (RD) December 1, 1851, (CLK) W.O. Young.

575) Second annual settlement of Martha A.V. Ewing, adm. of the estate of Samuel G. Ewing, dec. December term, 1851.

Monies Received: Carty Wells, attorney.

Monies Expended: Nancy Cottle. (RD) December 1, 1851, (CLK) W. O. Young.

576) First annual settlement of Robert M. Spalding, adm. of the estate of Thomas P. Norton, dec. January term, 1852.

Monies Expended: S. Smith, G. H. Edward, W. H. Danert.

(RD) January 5, 1852, (CLK) W. O. Young.

577) Third annual settlement of George L. Hardy, adm. of the estate of John N. Elsea, dec. November term, 1851, Rendered on January 5, 1852.

Monies Received: Benedict Elder.

Monies Expended: George Whitecotton; January 5, 1851 to Samuel Leake; On December 23, 1850 to Mary D. Redman; On January 5, 1852 to W. O. Young. (RD) January 6, 1852, (CLK) W. O. Young.

578) Second annual settlement of Ulysses Norton, adm. of the estate of Rachael Norton, dec. February term, 1852.

Monies Expended: On June 3, 1851 to George E. Frazer; On May 6, 1851 to E. W. Southworth for J. B. Newland; On January 30, 1852 on account of Dr. Bartlett; On February 4, 1851 to W. O. Yong; On March 15, 1851 to B. Ely; Mention of Dr. Newland. (RD) February 3, 1852, (CLK) W. O. Young.

579) First and final settlement of Ben A. Spalding, public administrator, of the estate of James C. Shafer, dec. February term, 1852.

Monies Received: William Crawford, Amos Hill, George Shaver, D. B. Kendrick, Mention of --- Williamson (previous administrator). (RD) March 1, 1852, (CLK) W. O. Young.

580) First settlement of James Hornback, adm. of the estate of Barbara C. Keith, dec. February term, 1852.

Monies Received: Sale Bill recorded on December 27, 1850; Monies received for cutting wheat from Mrs. Neal, Robert J. Rudisill, Turner G. Roost.

Monies Expended: William Maddox, James Glascock. (RD) March 1, 1852, (CLK) W. O. Young.

581) Second annual settlement of Ben A. Spalding, public administrator, of the estate of William Lambeth, dec. March Adjourned term, 1852.

Monies Expended: On March 17, 1851 to W. T. Cleaver, On March 4, 1851 to Thos. Cleaver, On May 6, 1851 to W. Wood, On August 21, 1852 to B. Epperson, W.L. Lofland. (RD) March 2, 1852, (CLK) W. O. Young.

582) First and final settlement of the estate of Robert C. Briggs, adm. with the will annexed for Robert Briggs, deceased. March term, 1852.

Monies Received: Edward Dunning.

Monies Expended: --- Hays, Mills & Menefee, A. Davidson, John K. Hawkins, W. T. Briggs, William Wise, W. O. Young, John Ralls. (RD) April 6, 1852, (CLK) W. O. Young.

583) Second annual settlement of Allen G. Gallaher, adm. of the estate of J. J. T. McElroy, dec. April term, 1852.

Monies Received: Sale of the negro Emavine (?).

Monies Expended: On May 3, 1851 to John Muldrow, On April 29, 1851 to William R. Campbell, on April 26, 1851 to J. P. Leake, On April 9, 1851 to W. O. Young, In 1852 to H. G.

Martin; In February, 1852 to Carter & Ely; In 1852 to J. R. Irvne; In 1851 to --- Snider. (RD) April 7, 1852, (CLK) W. O. Young.

584)   First annual settlement of Ulysses Norton, adm. of the estate of Fountain Kenney, dec. May term, 1852.

Monies Received: On May 22, 1852 from J. Wilson; On May 22, 1852 from the sale of property in Shelby Co., Mo.; On April 15, 1852 from the estate of T. P. Norton; On May 22, 1852 from J. Hagar; In September, 1851 from L. H. Gardner for the hire of a negro girl; In December, 1851 from B. H. Spalding for the hire of a negro girl; In December 1851 from Matthew Elliott for the hire of a negro girl; In April, 1852 from D. Briscoe.

Monies Expended: On June 6, 1851, July 7, 1851, and February 2, 1851 to B. M. Spalding, adm. of the estate of T. P. Norton; On March 1, 1852 to Joseph Henderson; On September 30, 1851 to Martin Leister; On June 6, 1851 to G. L. Hardy; On May 3, 1851 to John Hagar; On July 11, 1851 to J. Watson; On April 28, 1851 to J. P. Ament; On November 4, 1851 to A. F. Wayland; Receipt given by U. Norton, adm. of the estate of Rachael Norton, as dowry from the estate of T. P. Norton; On April 27, 1852 to D. O'Brien for the maintenance of Oren Kenney, minor heir of F. Kenney, dec. from April, 1851 to April, 1852; In June, 1851 reimbursement for expense of trip to Macon Co.; On March 1, 1851 to Dr. Lyle. (RD) May 4, 1852 to W. O. Young.

585)   Sixth and final settlement of Charles Rice, as surviving executor of the estate of Thomas Hicklin, dec. February term, 1852.

Monies Exepnded: Receipts paid to Robert W. Hicklin, Tho. B. Hicklin, and Otho B. Hicklin; On August 9, 1851 to John C. Briggs; On May 31, 1851 to John C. Briggs; On November 23, 1851 to John C. Briggs; On November 23, 1851 to S. W. Mayhall; On February 4, 1852 to J. P. Ament; On February 2, 1852 to John C. Briggs; On February 2, 1851 to W. O. Young; On February 2, 1852 to John Ralls; Mention of judgement against the estate of Otho Brashear, dec. (RD) May 5, 1852, (CLK) W. O. Young.

586)   Third and final settlement of James Culbertson, adm. of the estate of Frances A. Purdom, dec. June term, 1852.

Monies Expended: Jno. William, guardian of Emaline Prudom, and Hezekiah Purdom; On January 1, 1849 to J. B. Green; On February 22, 1849 to J. Sorey; On December 25, 1851 to W. O. Young. (RD) June 9, 1851, (CLK) W. O. Young.

587)   Third and final settlement of James Culbertson, adm. of the estate of Peter Smelser, dec. June term, 1852.

Monies Expended: N. T. Pierce; Matthew Smith; On June 9, 1852 to Eli W. Southworth; On December 30, 1851 to Samuel

Smith; On May 25, 1852 to J. Sosey; On March 24, 1852 to A. Ellis, J. W. Hawkins and W. O. Young; Susan Rice; John M. Kelly; J. D. Briggs; Henry Smelser. (RD) July 9, 1852, (CLK) W. O. Young.

588) Annual settlement of Luke W. Watkins, adm. of the estate of Hiram Whittmoore, dec. July term, 1852.

No names given. (RD) July 5, 1852, (CLK) W. O. Young.

589) First annual settlement of Charles G. Bulkley, adm. of the estate of Abner S. Clarke, dec. July term, 1852.

Monies Expended: On April 7, 1852 to Thomas Pierce; W. O. Young; A. Clemens. (RD) July 5, 1851, (CLK) W. O. Young.

590) Fourth and final settlement of Benjamin A. Spalding, late public administrator for the estate of James Lee, dec. July term, 1852.

Monies Expended: John Ralls, Carty Wills, Isaac Scare, John Jamison, S. K. and R. B. Caldwell, W. O. Young. (RD) July 5, 1992, (CLK) W. O. Young.

591) First annual settlement of John Boyers and James N. Smith, exrs. of the estate of Thomas Smith, dec. August term, 1852.

Monies Expended: Robert C. Briggs, guardian; James H. Jackson and wife; John L. Smith; John L. Smith, adm. of the estate of Stephen Smith, dec.; James Cooper and wife, Mary; Thomas L. Grimes; Eliza Bast; Nancy Smith; W. O. Young; Mary Cooper; Nancy Smith; Richard L. Warren; Walter Ellice; Silas M. Rosser; Ignacius Spalding; George L. Hardy; William O. Young; Orian Clemens; Ignacious A. Spalding; G. E. Frasier; Conrad R. Coonts; Levi Keithly; Samuel Smith; Lewis H. Gardner; On September 1, 1851 to J. S. Crosthwait; On September 2, 1851 Absalom Rice; On September 2, 1851 to E. A. Tapley; On September 2, 1851 to Livers & Hicklin; On October 6, 1851 to George Rice; On November 4, 1850 to John Biggs; On July 11, 1850 to W. Epperson; W. O. Young; S. K. Caldwell. (RD) August 3, 1852, (CLK) W. O. Young.

592) First annual settlement of James H. Ely, adm. of the estate of Joshua Ely, dec. August term, 1852.

Monies Received: Contract with John Alford due December 25, 1853.

Monies Expended: On March 23, 1852 to J. A. Spalding. (RD) August 3, 1852.

593) First annual settlement of John Rouse, adm. of the Gilliam King, dec. This is the second settlement with the Ralls Co. Court. August term, 1852.

Monies Received: In 1852 for cash received from the Crawford estate per suit in the Monroe Ct. et; On April 3, 1852 from Wm. Turner.

Monies Expended: On May 15, 1852 paid the Widow; On June 7, 1852 to the adm. of Allen Rouse; On April 3, 1853 to John A. Crawford; On July 17, 1852 to John Milton; On May 4, 1852 to W. I. Howell; On June 7, 1852 to W.O. Young. (RD) August 5, 1852, (CLK) W. O. Young.

594) First annual settlement of Amos Hill, adm. of the estate of Sarah Hill, dec. September term, 1852.

Monies Received: Sale of personal property on August 27, 1851.

Monies Expended: On August 9, 1852 to S. Baun; On August 27, 1851 to J. A. SpaldingOn February 4, 1851 to M. Leister; On February 3, 1851 to S. Wilson; On November 6, 1851 to John Miller; On August 27, 1851 to Wm. Crawford; On September 7, 1852 to William Young. (RD) September 6, 1852 to William O. Young.

595) First annual settlement of Charles G. Bulkey, adm. of the estate of Abner W. Clark, dec. September term, 1852.

Monies Expended: Widow's receipt. (RD) September 6, 1852. (CLK) William O. Young.

596) Second annual settlement of Norman Robinson, adm. of the estate of Benjamin Robinson, jr. dec. September term, 1852.

No names given. (RD) September 6, 1852. (CLK) William O. Young.

597) Second annual settlement of William Shuck, adm. of the estate of T--sey (?) Snider, dec. August term, 1852.

No names given. (RD) September 7, 1852, (CLK) William O. Young.

598) First annual settlement of William T. Briggs, exr. of the estate of Robert Briggs, dec. July term, 1852. (Note: This entry was crossed out in the original manuscript.)

Monies Expended: On March 2, 1852 to John C. Criggs; On March 2, 1852 to Robert Hagan; On March 22, 1852 to Benjamin M. Briggs; On June 2, 1852 to Gavin Brashear; On March 7, 1852 to Coleman D. Stone; On May 8, 1852 to Wm. O. Young; On March 9, 1852 to John Coons; On March 9, 1852 to Robert Hagar; On February 28, 1852 to B. M. Briggs; On February 28, 1852 to C. Carstarphen. (RD) None, (CLK) None.

599) Settlement given in No. 598 above is listed again. Same information is duplicated. (RD) October 4, 1852, (CLK) Wm. O. Young.

600) First annual settlement of Levi Keithly, adm. of the estate of Elvira Martin, dec. October term, 1852.

Monies Received: On April 1, 1852 from Wm. Collins.

Monies Expended: On July 7, 1851 to Wm. O. Young; On January 25, 1851 payment was made for coffin and burial clothes; On December 2, 1851 to Tyre A. Haden; On October 2, 1852 to George S. Hardy; On October 4, 1852 to Ezra Hunt. (RD) October 5, 1852, (CLK) William O. Young.

601) First annual settlement of Lovel Rouse, adm. of the estate of Allen Rouse, dec. October term, 1852.

Monies Received: Estate of G. King.

Monies Expended: On November 4, 1851 to S. Smith; On September 9, 1851 to W. O. Young; On April 29, 1851 to P. S. Dams; On February 15, 1852 to I. A. Quarles; On October 5, 1852 to Snider & Lyle; On November 4, 1851 to W. O. Young. (RD) October 5, 1852, (CLK) W. O. Young.

602) First annual settlement of Mary Gilbert, adm. of the estate of Austin Gilbert, dec. October term, 1852. Monies Expended: On October 6, 1851 to George C. Hays; On October 6, 1851 to P. F. Field; On October 6, 1851 to James Shahoney; On May 12, 1852 to James T. Matson; On January 15, 1952; On July 29, 1852 to John D. Field; On April 6, 1852 to Hiram Glasscock; On October 4, 1852 to Taylor Jones. (RD) October 6, 1852, (CLK) William O. Young.

603) Third and final settlement of the estate of Thomas A. Purdom, dec., and the second settlement by Samuel Smith, adm. debonis non (?). October term, 1852. (Note: Former administrator was C. Carstarphen.) Monies Expended: J. P. Ament, W. O. Young. (RD) October 7, 1852, (CLK) William O. Young.

604) Second annual settlement of James A. Emison, adm. of the estate of James Turley, dec. November term, 1852. Monies Expended: G.C. Hays, George Glascock, J. Jamison, T. Rodes, J. Krigbaum, J. R. Hawkins, S. W. Mayhall, J. Herlinger, S. Smith, S. K. Caldwell, J. A. H. Lampton, Clayton & Strode, Wm. K. Biggs, O. Clemens, John Ralls, G. Glascock, Allen Brown, W. C. Broughton, W. O. Young, E. Hawkins. (RD) November 1, 1852, (CLK) William O. Young.

605) Third annual settlement of William Stone, adm. of the estate of Susannah Riddle, dec. November term, 1852. Monies Expended: Sam. K. Caldwell, W. O. Young. John Ralls. (RD) ?, (CLK) ?

606) Second annual settlement of Nancy Conn, adm. of the will annexed by Francis Conn, dec. November term, 1852. Monies Received: Rent of land from W. W. Powell; rent of farm from P. C. Suttle; account against R. N. Woolfork. Monies Expended: T. M. Hendricks, J. R. Clayton, A. R. Maddox, Levi Hatchett, Martha L. Reading, F. T. Conn, On September 2, 1850 to A. Ellis, Absalom Ellis, David Clark, Miller Johnson (insolvent note), On November 11, 1850 to J. C. Briggs, On February 11, 1851 to John G. Gregory, On December 21, 1850 to Henry Smelser, On October 18, 1852 to Absalom Ellis, On November 6, 1850 to Absalom Ellis, On December 3, 1850 to Absalom Ellis, On March 6, 1851 to Absalom Ellis, On September --, 1849 to Tramuel Conn, On July 11, 1850 to --- Ament, On September --, 1851 to G. E. Frazier, On August 28, 1850 to F. Conn; On August 28, 1850 to William O. Conn, T. Conn, John Ralls, O. Clemens. (RD) November 1, 1852, (CLK) Wm. O. Young.

607) First annual settlement of John D. Biggs, adm. of

97

the estate of William E. Higgins, dec. November term, 1852.
No names given. (RD) November 2, 1852, (CLK) William O.
Young.
608) Third and final settlement of Wilkinson Crawford,
adm. of the estate of John M. Crawford, dec. November term,
1852.
Monies Expended: On November 5, 1849 to Dr. E.C. Redman;
On December 2, 1850 to McElroy & Frazier; In November, 1849
to James Turbo; Orion Clemens; W. O. Young. (RD) ?, (CLK) ?
609) Second annual settlement of William H. Smith, adm.
of the estate of John Herlinger, dec. November term, 1852.
Monies Expended: Jas. Gibbons; G. C. Hays, jr.; G. C.
hays, sr.; H. H. Crooks; H. Brown; Clayton & Strode; Jacob
Herlinger; E. W. Southworth; C. Carstarphen;J. W. Gallager;
Kercherval & Green. (RD) November 3, 1852, (CLK) William O.
Young.
610) First annual settlement of Fanny Shahoney, adm. of
the estate of James Shahoney, dec. December term, 1852.
No names given. (RD) December 20, 1852, (CL) William O.
Young.
611) Third and final settlement of George C. Muldrow,
adm. of the estate of Samuel Muldrow, dec. November term,
1852.
Monies Expended: J. P. Ament, E. W. Southworth, J. R.
Carter, L. Fagan, Wm. O. Young, John Ralls. (RD) December
22, 1852, (CLK) William O. Young.
612) First annual settlement of Peter C. Settle, exr. of
the estate of George Settle, dec. January term, 1853.
Monies Received: On August 30, 1851 for the hire of Eze-
kial.
Monies Expended: On December 24, 1851 to Meredith & Hawkins; On January 2, 1852 to Susan E. Turner; On January 20,
1852 to Hiram W. Glascock; On January 1, 1852 to Grayson
Dulin; On January 1, 1852 to J. K. Hawkins; On January 1,
1852 to Wm. O. Young; On January 1, 1852 to O. Clemens; On
December 24, 1851 to S. Davis; On October 4, 1851 to E. & G.
Hawkins; On April 7, 1852 to Anderson Teague; On April 7,
1852 to Susan E. Turner. (RD) January 3, 1853, (CLK) William
O. Young.
613) First annual settlement of John Ralls, adm. of the
estate of James Daulton, dec. January term, 1853.
Monies Received: James Glascok, R. Buchanan, John Ralls,
Wm. O. Young, William G. Daulton, H. C. Daulton, Thomas Win-
ters, John T. Daulton. (RD) January 3, 1853, (CLK) William
O. Young.
614) First annual settlement of John Ralls, adm. of the
Marquis Hall, dec. February term, 1853.
Monies Received: On account from Daniel Shivers in
California as reported by him; pork barrels in the store at

Dowling's in Hannibal.

Monies Expended: J. P. Ament, Sarah Hall (receipt for personal estate), Daniel Shiver. (RD) January 3, 1853, (CLK) William O. Young.

615) Third and final settlement of John M. Johnson, adm. of the estate of Joseph K. Johnson, dec. February term, 1853.

Monies Expended: --- O. Clemens, William O. Young, (RD) February 7, 1853, (CLK) William O. Young.

616) Second and final settlement of John T. Buzendine, surviving executer of the will of Lewis Buzendine, dec. January term, 1853.

Monies Expended: Wm. O. and W. S. Lofland, A. C. Hawkin's estate, S. W. Mayhall, Caldwell Purdom, R. B. Caldwell, E. W. Southworth, J. Ralls, Catherine Hankins. (RD) January 7, 1853.

617) Third and final settlement of Martha A. V. Ewing, adm. of the estate of Samuel G. Ewing, dec. February term, 1853.

Monies Expended: Gabriel Penn, Rueben Son. February term, 1853. (RD) February 7, 1853, (CLK) William O. Young.

618) Second annual settlement of John M. Mills and Charles W. Mills, August term, 1852.

Monies Expended: Allotment of slaves to James M. Mills, Widow Mary G. Mills, James M. Mills, Ch. W. Mills, Charles L. Mills, dec., Granville R. Mills, and James L. Mills; John Ralls, James Glascock. (RD) February 8, 1853, (CLK) Wm. O. Young.

619) First annual settlement of Eliza Smarr, adm. of the estate of Thomas Smarr, dec. February term, 1853.

Monies Received: Inventory was filed on January 6, 1852; Abner A. Smarr; J. S. Saunders; L. Garnett; J. R. Flowerree; rent of land; hire of three slaves.

Monies Expended: On April 14, 1852 to A. C. Hankins; On February 11, 1852 TO Dr. Hankins; On February 9, 1852 to --- Kaufman; On February 16, 1852 to --- Dawson; On January 8, 1852 to G. Bacon; On February 12, 1852 to E. and G. W. Hankins; On January 1, 1853 to Collins & Breeds; On February 1, 1852 to Curts & Lockwood; On December 6, 1851 to --- Smith; On January 13, 1853 to --- Blanchet; On May 29, 1852 to Samuel Smarr; On January 29, 1852 to Jno. W. Stavety. (RD) February 9, 1853, (CLK) William O. Young, (RD) February 9, 1853.

620) First annual settlement of John Ralls, adm. of the estate of Gersham Silver dec. February term, 1853.

Monies Received: Inventory filed October 6, 1851. Sale Bill filed October 6, 1851; --- Stillwell.

Monies Expended: On September 20, 1851 to Jn. K. Hankins; On September 20, 1851 to B. Stevens; On September 20,

1851 to P. C. Settle; On September 20, 1851 to Thos. I. Killen; On September 20, 1851 to H. A. Harris; On October 6, 1851 to John Ralls; On October 6, 1851 to Elijah Sims; On October 6, 1851 to Rebecca Haynes; On December 7, 1851 to Milleson Silver; On March 2, 1852 to Samuel Newlon (sic); On November 2, 1852 to Armstrong & Dawson; On August 3, 1852 to On January --, 1852 to Mary Silver; On February 8, 1853 to James M. Mills. (RD) February 10, 1853, (CLK) Wm. O. Young.

621) First annual settlement of Robert C. Briggs, adm. of the estate of Adam Bast, dec. March term, 1853.

Monies Received: On January 27, 1852 from James H. Ely for a note due on May 1, 1852.

Monies Expended: On January 27, 1852 to the Widow Eliza Bast; In March 1853 to the Widow and J. A. Spalding; On January 27, 1852 to I. W. Lewellen; On March 7, 1853 to William O. Young; On March 7, 1853 to John Ralls; On March 7, 1853 to Orion Clemens. (RD) March 7, 1853, (CLK) Wm. O. Young.

622) Second annual settlement of James Hornback, adm. of the estateof Barbara C. Keith, dec. March term, 1853.

Monies Expended: Kercheval & Green; Dr. McKalavay; John R. Floweree. (RD) March 7, 1853, (CLK) William O. Young.

623) Settlement of Thomas S. Grimes, as surviving partner of James Grimes, dec. March term, 1853. (RD) March 8, 1853, (CLK) William O. Young.

624) First annual settlement of Thomas S. Grimes, adm. of the estate of James Grimes, dec. March term, 1853.

Monies Received: Inventory filed March 3, 1851.

Monies Expended: John D. Briggs, -- Young, -- Clemens. (RD) March 8, 1853.

625) Second annual settlement of James Ely, adm. of the estate of William Ely, dec. March term, 1853.

Monies Expended: J. Abbay. (RD) March 8, 1853, William O. Young.

626) Second annual settlement of John Chitwood, adm. of the estate of Seth Chitwood, dec. February term, 1853.

Monies Expended: On October 29, 1852 to Amos Chitwood. (RD) February 8, 1853, (CLK) Wm. O. Young.

627) First annual settlement of Thomas I. Ellis, public adm. of the estate of John Bell, dec. February adjourned term, 1853.

Monies Received: One note on Lawrence Taliaferro now in the hands of H. A. Harris; Judgment against D. B. Young on Justice Harris' docket. (RD) April 4, 1853, (CLK) William O. Young.

628) First annual settlement of Julia Ann Silver, adm. of the estate of William Silver, dec. April term, 1853.

Monies Received: Ingram's note and interest from July 1, 1851; --- Lowe; --- Kercheval.

Monies Expended: J. S. Matthews, Wm. Hawkins, Shulse &

Davis, --- Gordon, John Ralls, --- Clemens, tuition for two children. (RD) April 4, 1853, (CLK) Wm. O. Young.

629) First annual settlement of Thomas S. Ellis, adm. Monies Received: Benjamin A. Spalding. (RD) April 4, 1853, (CLK) William O. Young.

630) First annual settlement of Thomas I. Ellis, adm. of the estate of John N. Elsea. February adjourned term, 1853. Monies Received: George L. Hardy, David Blue, R. Shick, J. I. Bradley, Wm. H. Perry. Monies Expended: S. Smith. (RD) April 4, 1853, (CLK) William O. Young.

631) First annual settlement of Thomas I. Ellis, adm. of the estate of Richard Boulware, dec. February adjourned term, 1853. Monies Received: From John I. Lyle for rent of farm; From Morton I. Lyle for rent of farm. Monies Expended: Saml. Smith. (RD) April 4, 1853, (CLK) William O. Young.

632) Second annual settlement of William T. Briggs, exr. of the estate of Robert Briggs, dec. April term, 1853. Monies Received: --- Conn, Mary I. Kelley. Monies Expended: On November 9, 1852 to J. Kelly; On November 9, 1852 to John C. Briggs; On November 12, 1852 to C. Carstarphen; On November 12, 1852 to Robert Hagan; On November 12, 1852 to Benjamin M. Briggs; On March 1, 1852 to R. C. Briggs; On November 8, 1852 to R. C. Briggs; On November 9, 1852 to Geo. L. Hardy; Paymetn to Wim. T. Briggs as distributor and guardian for Mary I. Wise. (RD) April 4, 1853, (CLK) William O. Young.

633) Fourth annual settlement of John D. Smith and Bartlett G. White, exr. of the last will and testament of Stephen McPherson, dec. February term, 1853. Monies Received: In August, 1850, from Joseph Hardy and Chs. Bohannon; Sam. Smith; Caleb Galliher; William Maddox; Wm. Newland. (RD) April 7, 1853, (CLK) William O. Young.

634) First annual settlement of William C. Splawn, adm. of the estate of John I. Ely, dec. May term, 1853. Monies Received: Sale bill filed April 6, 1852; S. B. Means. Monies Expended: In 1853 to A. A. Beshears; On April 29, 1852 to Dean & Garnett; On January 4, 1852 to John A. Steen; On September 3, 1852 to Hugh Emison; On February 4, 1853 to J. S. Crosthwait; On December 10, 1852 to Charles Rice; On March 23, 1853 to John K. Hawkins; On April 19, 1853 to J. S. Crosthwait. (RD) May 2, 1853, (CLK) William O. Young.

635) First annual settlement of Joseph W. Johnson, adm. of the estate of Richard Johnson, dec. May term, 1853. Monies Expended: On February 2, 1852 to A. Morrow. (RD) May 3, 1853, (CLK) William O. Young.

636) Second annual settlement of Ulysses Norton, adm. of the estate of Fountain Kenney, dec. May term, 1853.
Monies Received: From the estate of Th. R. Norton on February 2, 1852; From the hire of a negro girl in 1852 on January 1, 1853.
Monies Expended: On March 1, 1852 to John J. Lyle; On July 7, 1851 to Benjamin Ely; In September, 1852, to Samuel K. Caldwell; On September 7, 1851 to W. O. Young; On February 4, 1854 to R. M. Leake; In January, 1853, to James Kenney; Joshua Wilson. (RD) May 3, 1853, (CLK) Wm. O. Young.
637) Third and final settlement of Norman Robinson, adm. of the estate of Benjamin Robinson, jr., dec. May term, 1853.
Monies Expended: On march 28, 1853 to --- Oldemen, J. A. Aud and Daniel Herrin; On April 12, 1853 to Robert Spalding, E. E. Southworth, W. O. Young, --- Oldemen and John Ayres. (RD) May 3, 1853, (CLK) William O. Young.
638) Final settlement of Ulysses Norton, adm. of the estate of Rachael Norton, dec. May term, 1853.
Monies Expended: W. P. Norton, Wm. B. Norton, Minerva Spalding, O. Kenney, On April 3, 1853 to O. Clemens, On May 3, 1853 to W. O. Young. The slaves mentioned in the will were delivered to James J. Norton, Wm. B. Norton, and Wm. P. Norton. (RD) May 4, 1853, (CLK) William O. Young.
639) Second annual settlement of Charles G. Bulkey, adm. of the estate of Abner S. Clark, dec. June term, 1853.
Monies Expended: On March 1, 1852 to M. F. Brown; On March 21, 1853 to Michael M. Mason. (RD) June 6, 1853, (CLK) Wm. O. Young.
640) Second annual settlement of Charles G. Bulkey, adm. of the estate of Abner W. Clark, dec. July term, 1853.
(Note: There are two separate entries recorded and both are listed next to each other.)
Monies Received: James Painter, Henry Parks, John Dryden, Merdman (sic) Hightower.
Monies Expended: On April 4, 1853 to Jane Clark. (RD) July 5, 1853, (CLK) Wm. O. Young.
641) First annual settlement of John S. Smith, adm. of the estate of Stephen T. Smith, dec. June term, 1853.
Monies Expended: On February 5, 1853 to R. C. Briggs, adm. of A. Bast; On August 15, 1852 to John Coons; On August 7, 1852 to Young & Clemens; On September 6, 1852 to E. W. Southworth. (RD) June 6, 1853, (CLK) William O. Young.

104

BRICE, 28 42 57 67 68 69
BRIGGS, 2 3 28 32 61 70
  79 81 90 93-97 100 102
BRISCO, 4
BRISCOE, 3 5 9 10 12 28
  55 58 64 71 80 86-88 94
BRIZENDINE, 21 75
BROCKMAN, 17 43
BRONAUGH, 49 60 66 71
BROOKS, 5 26 28 42 44
BROROUGH, 41
BROTHERS, 5 8 16 30 49 60
BROUGHS, 39
BROUGHTON, 69 81 97
BROWN, 1 2 4 5 8 9 12 14
  16 19 21-24 34 35 37-40
  42 45 47 48 51-53 55 56
  60 62-66 68 73-75 78 80
  82 87-90 97 98 102
BROWNELL, 72 82 85
BROWNING, 16
BRYAN, 42 85
BRYANT, 11 15
BUCHANAN, 13 21 27 31 32
  34 36 41 49-51 53-56
  58-68 70-74 76 78-80
  82-86 88 89 91 98
BUCHANNAN, 37 39 40 41 42
  44 46 47
BUCHANNON, 18 37 38 72
BUCHANON, 20
BUCK, 49
BUCKANNON, 5
BUCKHANNAN, 25
BUCKHANNON, 20 39
BUCKMAN, 45
BUCKNER, 16 22 53 63
BUFORD, 2 8 12 20 21 25
  26 28 31 34 35 40 49 50
  52 53 56 57 63-65 84 88
  89
BULKEY, 96 102
BULKLEY, 95
BULL, 27
BULLER, 50
BUR, 28
BURCH, 92
BURFORD, 26

BURNS, 1
BUSBY, 2
BUTLER, 24 57 87
BUZENDINE, 99
BYANT, 15
BYARS, 14
BYERS, 66 77
BYRNE, 5
CACTS, 38
CALDDWELL, 62
CALDWELL, 1-3 5 6 8-10 12
  13 16 19 27 35 38 39 42
  43 45 50 52-55 57 58 60
  61 63-66 68-71 73 74
  76-92 95 97 99 102
CALHOUN, 9 60 83 90
CALHOURN, 14
CAMA, 1
CAMBRICK, 9
CAMERON, 22 27
CAMPBELL, 10 13 16 17 22
  23 31 38 41 48 50 57-60
  63 66 69 72 78 84 89 93
CAMRON, 17
CANAWAY, 16
CANNON, 77
CANTERBERRY, 25
CANTERBURY, 22
CAPEHART, 91
CARISLE, 4
CARLISLE, 7
CARLSON, 13
CARSIES, 21
CARSON, 2 4 6 7 8 19 24
  31 50 52 92
CARSTAPHEN, 14
CARSTARPEHEN, 5 9 47
CARSTARPHEN, 1 2 4 5 7 8
  12 14 19 23 24 27 34 35
  38 45 48 50 52 57 60 66
  70 71 74 81 89 92 96-98
  101
CARTER, 3 4 13 26 27 33
  37 45 55 65 76 94 98
CARTMELL, 59
CARTMILL, 10
CARTWELL, 13
CARTWILL, 15 21 75

106

GANT, 3 4 12
GARDINER, 21 39 43
GARDNER, 12 39 87 90 94
  95
GARICK, 18
GARNET, 10 22
GARNETT, 4 27 37 99 101
GARRENT, 6
GARRET, 77
GARRETT, 31
GARRISH, 24 27 32 66
GARRISON, 50
GARTH, 75
GASH, 8
GASTON, 6 13
GATEWOOD, 12 86
GATSON, 8 13 59 64 77
GAUNT, 8
GEARY, 85
GEERY, 49 74
GENTRY, 39 40 43 45 49 50
  59 69 71
GERARD, 49 58 64 82
GERICK, 23
GERNSAY, 16
GERRARD, 27 55 70 87
GERRISH, 24 84
GIBBONS, 98
GILBERT, 29 54 60 64 74
  97
GILLESPIE, 7 19 30 62 76
GLASCK, 3
GLASCOCK, 1-10 12-16 19-
  22 24 25 27 31-33 35
  38-41 44 45 47 48 51-58
  60 61 63 65 66 68-70 72
  74 75 77 78 80 81 86-91
  93 97-99
GLASCOK, 98
GLASSCOCK, 97
GLEN, 1
GLENN, 3 7 9 11 14
GLOVER, 36 43 50 66 69 70
  72
GOODLOW, 4
GOODWIN, 67
GORDON, 101
GORE, 14 15 18 20 26 31

GORE (continued)
  32 40 62 63 71 81
GOVNY, 88
GRAHAM, 16
GRAN, 22
GRANT, 4 8 10 13 15
GRAVES, 88
GRAY, 1 22 44
GREATHOUSE, 9 46 58 59 81
  87
GREEN, 22 25 27 38 44 60
  87 94 98 100
GREGORY, 38 55 56 77 97
GRIFFIN, 7 8 26 69 75 81
  82
GRIFFITH, 17 79
GRIMES, 46 95 100
GULUAC, 59
GUNN, 45
HA, 46
HADEN, 2 3 6 15 26 29 33
  41 44 48 50 53 74 77 87
  96
HAGAN, 52 60 61 62 67 68
  82 83 101
HAGAR, 43 44 66 70 71 73
  80 91 94
HAGEN, 96
HAGER, 1 5 6 70
HAINES, 15 17
HAKINS, 60
HALDEBECK, 19
HALEY, 5
HALL, 11 15 21 61 64 77
  78 98 99
HALLS, 10
HALSEY, 33 61
HAMILTON, 47 52
HAMPTON, 19 20 51
HANDON, 15
HANKINS, 99
HANNA, 15
HANS, 59
HANSBOROGUH, 18
HANSBOROUGH, 24 29 34 41
HANSBROUGH, 34
HANT, 2
HARBINGER, 91

109

LAMB, 25 39 42 43 51 58
LAMBETH, 89 93
LAMPKIN, 33 75 78
LAMPTON, 53 57 60 63 66
  83 92 97
LANE, 1 2 3 40 61
LASEY, 18
LAWRENCE, 40
LAYNE, 12 35 43 79
LEACH, 36
LEAGUE, 85
LEAK, 21
LEAKE, 19 21 23 24 26 29
  30 31 36 39 42 46 52 53
  60-62 67-71 76 77 80 81
  83 87-90 93 102
LEAR, 18 23
LEDFORD, 2 3 5-8 12 14 24
  28 32 55 62 68 80 81 86
  88
LEE, 14 18 19 23 29 67 95
LEEK, 14
LEFEVER, 6
LEFLAND, 5
LEISTER, 88 94 96
LENEY, 15
LEONARD, 26 33 41 48
LETTER, 24
LETTR, 17
LEVERING, 22
LEVERS, 12
LEWELLEN, 7 62 70 83 87
  100
LIGHT, 85
LIGHTE, 66
LILLARD, 32
LINEY, 10
LING, 31
LINNEY, 16
LIPSCOMB, 36
LITER, 53 57 67 68 70 72
  79 80 81
LITERS, 77 89
LITTLE, 27 39 41 56 69
LIVERS, 3 95
LMARR, 22 74
LOCKWOOD, 3 59 99
LOFLAND, 1 2 9 16 20 30

LOFLAND (continued)
  39 48 52 92 93 99
LOFTTAN, 24
LONG, 31 33 52
LOVERRING, 22
LOW, 17 23 44 52
LOWE, 100
LYAGER, 27
LYLE, 1 6 9 13 14 19 20
  29 45 55 58 60 73 83 94
  97 101 102
LYLES, 49
LYNCH, 6 14 16 26 29 31
  32 33 39 40 62 71 83
LYONS, 34 35 45 53 58 75
  87 88
M'CREARY, 27
M'CUNE, 65
M'ELROY, 89
M'EROY, 25
M'FARLAND, 75
M'GAW, 27
M'GOWEN, 27
M'GOWN, 28
M'KAY, 7 24 26 32 34 64
  86
M'KEE, 5
M'MURTY, 27
M'PHERSON, 7 32 51
M'QUIE, 80
MACE, 41 62 75
MACKAY, 39
MADDOX, 30 38 46 52 54 62
  74 80 83 90 93 97 101
MAGEES, 67
MAGRUDER, 15
MAHALL, 11
MAHAN, 29
MAJIN, 91
MAN, 45
MAPIN, 3
MAPPIN, 1
MARCUS, 56
MARGIN, 40
MARKLE, 8 16 25 28 52
MARKLES, 25
MARKS, 72
MARQUIMS, 55

113

SHELL, 74
SHELLTON, 11
SHELLY, 44
SHEPARD, 16
SHIBLEY, 12
SHICK, 77 101
SHIELDS, 14 17 86
SHIVER, 99
SHIVERS, 98
SHOHONEY, 5 13
SHOHONG, 29
SHOHONNEY, 44
SHOHONY, 24 30
SHROPSHIRE, 5
SHROTER, 59
SHUCK, 31 70 91 96
SHULSE, 3 56 62 65 100
SHUTE, 89
SHUTTS, 21
SILER, 51 52
SILVER, 73 99 100
SIMMITTS, 3
SIMS, 3 16 55 100
SINCLAIR, 3 4
SINCLEAR, 13 49
SINKCLEAR, 88
SINKLEAR, 62 70 82
SIPPS, 63
SISK, 28 78 79
SKINNER, 75
SLATERY, 67
SLAVE, Ailsey 67 Albert
   75 Alice 84 Bob 66
   Burr 81 Charles 92
   Charlotte 62 Daniel 3
   Delila 92 Dinah 6 Eliza
   58 67 84 Emerson 56
   Fanny 92 Jack 25 92
   James 56 Jim 47 Joe 65
   John 76 92 Judah 66
   Liddy 3 Little Jim 75
   Littleton 92 Lucinda 58
   Mariah 81 Martha 58
   Mary 58 67 84 Mead 66
   Miles 65 Milla 1 Moses
   1 3 Rachael 25 Richard
   58 67 84 Robert 67 84
   Robin 58 Sam

SLAVE (continued)
   (Alias Samuel) 92 Sarah
   75 Scott 56 Sidney 1
   Thomas 56 Tobi 66
   Warren 62 Wash 18 23
   Washington 18 47
SLOSS, 24 28
SLOSSIN, 9
SLOSSON, 2 8 11 15 25 26
   27 28 37 49 54 57 84
SLUTTER, 38
SMALL, 21 28 36 45 60
SMALLT, 57
SMARR, 99
SMELSER, 1 72 79 80 89 94
   95 97
SMELSON, 30 31
SMELSTER, 2
SMESLER, 69
SMIS, 77
SMITH, 1-4 6 12 16 17 20
   21 26-28 30 36-39 42-47
   50-52 56 57 61-64 66
   68-72 74-76 78-80 82-88
   90-92 94 95 97-99 101
   102
SMIZER, 45
SNEED, 57 62 70 82
SNELL, 44
SNIDER, 43 60 63 73 77 91
   94 96 97
SNODGRASS, 86
SNYDER, 43
SOASEY, 47
SOMERS, 90
SON, 99
SONGRAM, 47
SOREY, 94
SOSEY, 18 21 23 45 46 48
   52 53 58 69 95
SOUTH, 78
SOUTHAN, 67 84
SOUTHWORTH, 36-45 51 54-
   59 61 62 64-68 71 73 75
   76 78 83-85 88-94 98 99
   102
SOWERS, 83
SOX, 14 22

117

Other Heritage Books by Sherida K. Eddlemon:

Missouri Genealogical Records and Abstracts:
Volume 1: 1766-1839
Volume 2: 1752-1839
Volume 3: 1787-1839
Volume 4: 1741-1839
Volume 5: 1755-1839
Volume 6: 1621-1839
Volume 7: 1535-1839

Missouri Genealogical Gleanings 1840 and Beyond, Volumes 1-9

1890 Genealogical Census Reconstruction: Mississippi, Volumes 1 and 2

1890 Genealogical Census Reconstruction: Missouri, Volumes 1-3

1890 Genealogical Census Reconstruction: Ohio, Volume 1
(with Patricia P. Nelson)

1890 Genealogical Census Reconstruction: Tennessee, Volume 1

A Genealogical Collection of Kentucky Birth and Death Records

Callaway County, Missouri, Marriage Records: 1821 to 1871

Cumberland Presbyterian Church, Volume One: 1836 and Beyond

Dickson County, Tennessee Marriage Records, 1817-1879

Genealogical Abstracts from Missouri Church Records and
Other Religious Sources, Volume 1

Genealogical Abstracts from Tennessee Newspapers, 1791-1808

Genealogical Abstracts from Tennessee Newspapers, 1803-1812

Genealogical Abstracts from Tennessee Newspapers, 1821-1828

Tennessee Genealogical Records and Abstracts, Volume 1: 1787-1839

Genealogical Gleanings from New York Fraternal Organizations
Volumes 1 and 2

Index to the Arkansas General Land Office, 1820-1907
Volumes 1-10

Kentucky Genealogical Records and Abstracts, Volume 1: 1781-1839

Kentucky Genealogical Records and Abstracts, Volume 2: 1796-1839

Lewis County, Missouri Index to Circuit Court Records, Volume 1, 1833-1841

Missouri Birth and Death Records, Volumes 1-4

Morgan County, Missouri Marriage Records, 1833-1893

Our Ancestors of Albany County, New York, Volumes 1 and 2

Our Ancestors of Cuyahoga County, Ohio, Volume 1
(with Patricia P. Nelson)

Ralls County, Missouri Settlement Records, 1832-1853

Records of Randolph County, Missouri, 1833-1964

Ten Thousand Missouri Taxpayers

*The "Show-Me" Guide to Missouri: Sources for
Genealogical and Historical Research*

CD: Dickson County, Tennessee Marriage Records, 1817-1879

*CD: Index to the Arkansas General Land Office, 1820-1907
Volumes 1-10*

CD: Missouri, Volume 3

CD: Tennessee Genealogical Records

CD: Tennessee Genealogical Records, Volumes 1-3

www.ingramcontent.com/pod-product-compliance
Lightning Source LLC
Chambersburg PA
CBHW060403090426
42734CB00011B/2247